SUE LAWRENCE'S
Book of Baking

SUE LAWRENCE'S
Book of Baking

GLORIOUS BREADS, BISCUITS, CAKES AND TARTS

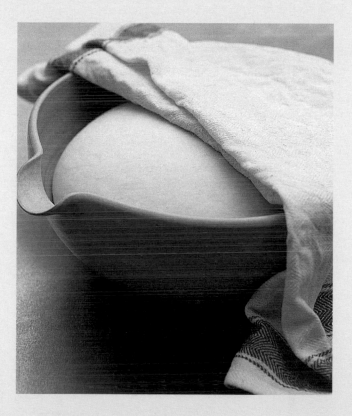

headline

For Hilary Blackford, friend and culinary soul mate.

Also by Sue Lawrence
Sue Lawrence's Scottish Kitchen
Scots Cooking
Entertaining at Home in Scotland
On Baking
On Salads
Feasting on Herbs
The *Sunday Times* Cookbook

Note: cup measurements give American volumes

Thanks to the following for supplying the props for the photo shoot:
Divertimenti (www.divertimenti.co.uk);
EDE & NIA (www.edeandnia.co.uk);
Her House (+44 20 7689 0808);
Jonathan's Kitchenwares at
Camden Passage (+44 20 7359 4560);
Karin Eriksson (www.karindesign.co.uk);
Labour and Wait (+44 20 7729 6253);
Vessel (www.vesselgallery.com)

Copyright © 2004 Sue Lawrence
Photographs Copyright © 2004 Siân Irvine

The right of Sue Lawrence to be identified as the Author of the Work has been asserted by her in accordance with the Copyright, Designs and Patents Act 1988.

First published in 2004
by HEADLINE BOOK PUBLISHING

10 9 8 7 6 5 4 3 2 1

Cataloguing in Publication Data is available from the British Library

ISBN 0 7553 1211 2

Designed by Isobel Gillan
Photography by Siân Irvine
Home Economist Maxine Clark
Styled by Victoria Allen

Set in Bliss and Scala
Printed and bound in Italy by Canale & C.S.p.A

HEADLINE BOOK PUBLISHING
A division of Hodder Headline
338 Euston Road
London NW1 3BH

www.headline.co.uk
www.hodderheadline.com

Contents

INTRODUCTION

It is 9.55 a.m. and the Church Fair is due to open at 10.00 a.m. Behind the piles of neatly labelled and priced fruit loaves, pies, Victoria sponges and home-made bread, we – the stall-holders – are trying not to panic. For Mrs Mackie has not yet turned up. And despite the cornucopia of cakes and jam piled up on our stall, if Mrs M. does not arrive, there will be a great deal of tut-tutting. It has never happened before, but it is easy to anticipate the outcry.

For Mrs M. makes shortbread, and the entire fair wants some. It is not just any shortbread; it is the very best in Christendom. Indeed, the queues that form whenever the hordes stampede to our stall are nothing to do with Mrs Smith's chocolate cakes or Miss Marshall's three-fruit marmalade; it is all down to the shortbread.

One minute to go, the doors are flung open and in rushes Mrs Mackie (couldn't find the back door keys). The relief from the Cake and Candy Stall is almost tangible; it is at times like this we thank the Lord there is no alcohol permitted within the hallowed walls of the kirk, otherwise we might have hit the bottle. But no, all is well with the world. Let the people in.

And this predilection for shortbread – and indeed all aspects of home-baking – is not confined to church fairs or school sales. Neither is it confined to my home in Scotland; although, ever since I was a child, home-baking has played a vital role in my life. And by this I don't mean grand iced cakes for birthdays or three-tiered cake stands piled high with dainty scones and fancy cakes on special occasions. For me baking was part of every day: coming home from school to the rich, warm aroma and tantalising sight of a treacle scone warm from the oven, a scotch pancake fresh from the girdle or a sultana cake cooling on the rack. It was comforting and delicious. It was also – and still is – the most generous form of cookery. Think about it: when did you last bake a cake all for yourself?

Nowadays priorities seem to have shifted in some homes and good old-fashioned home-baking is often supplanted by so-called low-fat processed food with dubious ingredients. But although there can be a fairly high fat and sugar content in many home-baked goods, at least you – the home baker – are the arbiter of how much sugar, butter and salt go in. If you want to add less sugar to your scone, then do so. Home-made differs enormously from mass-produced and factory-baked goods, where cheap, refined ingredients including unhealthy hydrogenated fats and unnecessary preservatives are added to increase shelf life and lower the price. Home-baking, in contrast, invariably involves quality ingredients (unsalted butter, unrefined sugar, unbleached flour, pure vanilla extract, organic eggs) and perhaps a little effort.

I understand that the effort – and the time factor – worries some people, but consider just how long it takes to produce a scone: five minutes to rustle up and ten minutes to bake. Flapjacks are five minutes to prepare and 25 minutes to bake. By baking these yourself, you not only avoid commercial additives, you can also add healthy nuts, seeds or dried fruits to boost the nutritional value. It is also hugely therapeutic: madly knead a batch of bread dough and the stresses and strains of life will disappear. Gently roll out pastry to make an apple pie and you may even find yourself forgetting why on earth you started that ridiculous argument with your partner. It is also a great way to both entertain and involve children, for table-bashing kneading is something they love; icing pretty pictures on fairy cakes is something all ages can do.

Although some cooks imagine there are special skills required for baking (there are cooks who can bone a quail in two minutes flat but are terrified of baking a cake), I can assure you there is no fundamental difference between making soup and baking a brownie. Except that, with soups you can – within reason – sling in some leftovers, say herbs or vegetables, for extra flavour. With baking, you do need to follow the basic measurements, adhere to the size of cake tin and, of course, stick rigidly to the oven temperature. But once you have mastered a basic muffin, loaf or tart, you can add in optional extras according to taste.

One final point about home-baking: your cake might not resemble those synthetic supermarket offerings with their perfectly

straight edges, level tops and garish dayglo orange icing. Do not forget, however, this is a Good Thing. Your cake might look rather more rustic than shop bought, but that is the point; it is the intrinsic allure of home-made. To use the old-fashioned term, it is handcrafted – lovingly and happily. Because, as well as the time taken – and quality ingredients you have put in – you have also made something in an utterly selfless frame of mind. And if you have no takers right now (difficult to imagine), then squirrel some away in the freezer, ready to bring out later to share with others. Why? It simply tastes so good.

Sue Lawrence

INGREDIENTS

Sugar It's not fashionable but I start by laying my cards on the table and declaring that I love sugar; always have done since pinching sugar lumps when out for tea and my mum wasn't looking – or dipping raw rhubarb from the garden into bowls of the white stuff with my sister in early summer. Nowadays I only ever use unrefined sugar, however. Although it is nutritionally more or less the same as white refined sugar, all unrefined sugars contain trace elements of various minerals; as a general rule the darker the sugar, the more health benefits there are. There are also far more nuances of flavour, whether it is the fudgy taste of light muscovado or the treacle-toffee taste of dark muscovado (my favourite). There is so much refined sugar in processed foods, I firmly believe that a little natural, unrefined sugar in your home-baking is far better than the hidden sugars (and salt and dodgy fats) in a regular diet of processed foods.

And can I end by saying that, although I eat home-baking every single day – always have done – I still have good teeth and have always been the same shape (just a little taller than childhood rhubarb days).

Flour All flour is the same, isn't it? So why do you need to pay more than the cost of the cheapest bag in the supermarket? Well for a start, you want to use unbleached flour if possible. Why buy flour that has been chemically bleached if there are other options? Choose traditionally stoneground flours if possible, again because they are pure and natural and also because they have bags more flavour. Chemically bleached flours can also give simple baked goods an 'off', somehow metallic flavour. And when you see the word 'stoneground', do not immediately think, smirking unwittingly, that you are not ready to don your sandals and eat leaden wholemeal bread. Shipton Mill, for example, mills fine stoneground flours such as ciabatta flour, soft pastry and cake flour and self-raising flours, all organic.

For breads, use a strong flour, with a high protein content (10–14 per cent); and use a regular plain flour (8–10 per cent) for most pastries, soda breads and all sorts of baked goods such as biscuits, gingerbreads and brownies, traditionally risen with either bicarbonate of soda or baking powder. Incidentally, always sift flours, especially if adding baking powder or soda, to enhance lightness and also to ensure the powder is evenly distributed. Self-raising flour, around since the 1920s, is handy as the raising agents are already added.

Fats Always butter, never margarine is my rule. (And only unsalted butter, apart from making shortbread, when slightly salted is used.) Although margarine used to be considered the healthier option as it is lower in saturated fats, some soft margarines and spreads are made with hydrogenated fats which convert some of the unsaturated fats into trans-fats. And the latter, when used in food processing, have been linked with some degenerative illnesses. As a general rule, if a spread contains hydrogenated fats it will probably contain trans-fats. There are olive oil spreads which contain no trans-fats, however, so check out the tub of spread before buying.

It is advocated that margarine makes the lightest cakes and I do not deny it; this is because margarines are whipped up during the hydrogenation and blending process. But provided you beat the butter thoroughly, until pale – often with the sugar – before adding eggs, flour and so on, you too will have a light cake.

And as for flavour: good butter or refined margarine? There's no competition. The true flavour of butter wins hands down over margarine, with its refined, unnatural taste, every time. Olive oil can also be used in certain recipes, and as with butter, use the best – extra virgin – but not an overtly peppery one.

Some pastry recipes stipulate 'white fats' or 'shortening' in order to give a crisp, short texture. Again, most white fats are hydrogenated, so I would avoid and opt, as usual, for butter. Many pastry cooks swear by lard which also gives a very flaky pastry, but I prefer the purity of butter. Above all, avoid margarines with hydrogenated fats.

Eggs I always use free-range eggs, organic if possible. And I never use eggs straight from the fridge, but always have them ready at room temperature. (You never can tell when the urge to bake will strike.) But I do live in a Victorian house in Scotland and so my kitchen is cold for most of the year. But yours is perhaps normal temperature and so refrigeration is advisable. Bring them to room temperature first – very cold eggs can cause the mixture to curdle.

Chocolate 'Best quality' chocolate is specified in all baking: the difference to the taste is incomparable. Good quality chocolate means that dark chocolate should have over 50 per cent cocoa solids, but I think over 60 per cent is best. For recipes in this book, unless otherwise specified, aim for between 60 and 70 per cent cocoa solids. Dark chocolate with cocoa solids over 75 per cent is almost too bitter for baking and you may need to up the sugar content. Milk chocolate ought to have over 30 per cent cocoa solids and for white chocolate, ensure it is the very best quality you can afford, as there are some overly sweet sickly bars out there.

Some of my favourite brands for dark, milk and white chocolate are: Valrhona, Callebaut, Green & Black's and Lindt; Lindt's milk chocolate is also very handy to nibble on, to help concentrate the mind, while baking.

To melt chocolate, break up into small pieces and either place in a heatproof bowl over a pan of gently simmering water or put in a microwaveable bowl and heat in the microwave on a Medium setting until almost melted.

Citrus fruits Use unwaxed if possible; otherwise scrub first.

Yeast Fresh yeast is a pleasure to use but since it can be difficult to find, I have given all recipes with fast-action or easy-blend dried yeast. But if you can find fresh yeast, buy it (it freezes well) and use 15g/$^{1}/_{2}$ oz fresh yeast for every 7g/$^{1}/_{4}$ oz sachet of fast-action dried yeast. But with fresh yeast you need to blend it first with a little tepid water and a pinch of sugar then add to the flour and other ingredients after 10–15 minutes or when it has begun to froth.

Honey Opt for pure honey, preferably one with the bee-keeper's name on the label, for the best flavour. I particularly love heather honey or any of the spring or summer blossom honeys. If it is a set honey, melt gently by placing the opened jar in a microwave on Medium for a couple of turns.

Syrup and Treacle Golden syrup and black treacle are easily measured out if you first dip the spoon into boiling water or very lightly oil the spoon; or flour your scales beforehand.

Oatmeal Porridge oats are not the same as oatmeal, something often unclear in the UK and compounded by the fact that in America, porridge is often referred to as simply 'oatmeal'. Oatmeal (the real thing) can be bought in four grades – fine, medium, coarse and pinhead, the latter being the most nubbly, nutty cut. Fine and medium oatmeal are best in pastry and scones; and medium or coarse add texture to gingerbread, biscuits and oatcakes. Porridge oats (regular or jumbo) are rolled oats that have been partially steamed and so have less flavour than proper oatmeal. They are used in flapjacks where speed is the order of the day. (To cook porridge with 100 per cent pinhead oatmeal takes some 30 minutes, unlike the 5 minutes using rolled – porridge – oats. But do try making porridge with pinhead for the very best flavour and texture.)

Nuts Use up quickly if you are buying them already shelled, as they can go rancid. A quick toasting improves their taste but ensure they are completely cool before using in baking. Since nuts contain no cholesterol and are jam-packed with essential nutrients, add them, coarsely chopped, to biscuits, brownies and flapjacks for an added health boost – and extra flavour.

Vanilla Only ever buy pure vanilla extract, which is expensive but you only need a few drops. Look out for Madagascar vanilla extract for general baking; and you can use pure vanilla bean paste in cheesecakes (and of course ice creams). Avoid cheap vanilla essences as they are artificially flavoured.

Breads

Of all the forms of baking, surely bread is the most fascinating. Ever since the Egyptians discovered natural fermentation from airborne yeasts, then invented ovens to bake leavened breads, there has been a huge variety of loaves kneaded, left to rise, baked, admired and devoured. Whenever I am in another country I seek out the local loaf: in central Finland I enjoyed *kalakukko*, a hearty rye loaf filled with tiny whole fish and bacon that had been buried in straw in a barn all winter since outside was colder than a freezer. In eastern Turkey, I watched flatbreads being rolled out and baked on a large upturned pan over an open fire; we then ate them filled with curd cheese and fresh herbs. The exquisite taste in Brazil of little puffy cheese rolls made from cassava flour will never leave me. But even a basic loaf made with nothing other than unbleached flour, yeast and water – and a little bit of time – can be utterly memorable. We may not be able to live on bread alone, but I for one could not live without it ∎

A CLASSIC LOAF

This basic recipe can be modified depending on taste, with different flours or the addition of nuts or seeds. But it is so fabulous as it is, made with quality ingredients, I prefer to keep this one as it is: simple and delicious.

MAKES 2 LOAVES

700g/1 lb 9 oz/6 cups unbleached strong white flour, sifted

7g/$\frac{1}{4}$ oz sachet of fast-action/easy-blend dried yeast

2 teaspoons salt

1 Mix the flour and yeast in a bowl with the salt. Make a well in the centre and slowly pour in enough tepid water (about 450ml/16 fl oz/2 cups) to make a fairly soft dough.

2 Using floured hands, bring the dough together and turn out on to a floured surface. Knead for 10 minutes until smooth, regularly sprinkling lightly with flour (I use a flour shaker). The dough should be soft and shiny but not too sticky.

3 Place in an oiled bowl and cover with clingfilm. Leave in a warm place for 1–2 hours until almost doubled.

4 Oil two baking sheets. Knock back the dough, divide into two and shape into loaves. Place on the baking sheets and cover with oiled clingfilm. Leave to rise again in a warm place for about 45 minutes. The dough is ready when it does not spring back when gently pressed with your finger. Meanwhile, preheat the oven to 230°C/450°F/Gas 8.

5 Slash the top lightly with a knife to form slits then dust lightly with flour and bake for 20–25 minutes, or until the base sounds hollow when tapped. Alternatively, use the lower-oven method (see Bread Tip 15 on page 17): preheat the oven to 180°C/350°F/Gas 4. Place the bread in the oven and immediately increase the temperature to 220°C/425°F/Gas 7. Bake for 25–30 minutes, then remove to a wire rack to cool.

Variations

■ Substitute a quarter of the white flour with rye flour for a denser rye loaf; or substitute half of the white with granary flour for a lighter granary loaf.

■ Add 100g/3$\frac{1}{2}$ oz/$\frac{3}{4}$ cup chopped nuts or stoned, chopped olives, or 55g/2 oz/$\frac{1}{2}$ cup sunflower or pumpkin seeds to the dough for a change.

AGA BREAD

When my friend Hils bought an Aga I needed little excuse to visit her in her cottage in Gloucestershire to do some baking. Amid the usual delightful chaos of our six teenagers wandering in at strange hours requiring food, I realised what a brilliant concept the Aga is, since you don't have to think about Stage One in regular baking which is Switching On the Oven; with an Aga it is always hot and ready. Hils and I spent a blissful day baking, with odd snippets of advice from her dear offspring. Christopher suggested adding more water to the bread dough, Oliver more salt – and when the bread was out of the oven and we were devouring it, Simon's input was most apt: why on earth didn't we make more?

MAKES 1 LOAF

700g/1 lb 9 oz/6 cups unbleached strong white flour

7g/$\frac{1}{4}$ oz sachet of fast-action/easy-blend dried yeast

2 teaspoons salt

1 Sift the flour in a bowl with the yeast and salt, and stir well.

2 Make a well in the centre and very slowly pour in about 568ml/1 pint/2$\frac{1}{2}$ cups lepid water, enough to combine to a soft dough. It will be sticky, but remember: the wetter the dough, the better the bread.

3 Using floured hands, tip the dough on to a floured surface and knead for about 10 minutes, flouring lightly as you knead.

4 Place in a lightly oiled bowl and cover with clingfilm. Leave to rise for about an hour near the warmth of the Aga until the dough has more or less doubled in size. Knock back the dough then knead again for a minute or so. Butter a baking sheet. Shape the dough into a long oval and place on the baking sheet. Cover with oiled clingfilm and leave in a warm place for a further 30 minutes, or until puffed up. Remove the clingfilm, snip along the top of the loaf and dust with flour.

5 To bake, place the grid shelf on the floor of the roasting oven and place the baking sheet on top. Bake for 25–30 minutes, or until golden brown. It will sound hollow when tapped underneath. Remove to a wire rack and leave to cool completely before slicing.

BREAD-MACHINE LOAVES

Right, here I lay my cards on the (bread-making) table. I had never been a fan of bread machines. I was waiting to be convinced that they produce better bread than home-baked. To me there seemed to be a touch of Toys for the Boys about them, since so many males of the household enjoy using them.

Having said all that, I appreciate that all the factors I adore about making bread from scratch – the unpredictability of it all with each loaf having its own definite character; the joyful sight of dough rising in the airing cupboard; the mess of floury hands and board; the therapeutic effect of kneading for 10 minutes with the radio on and all the cares of the world offloading from me through my table-bashing – may not appeal to everyone.

Since early forays into the world of bread machines, I never found a loaf that was truly memorable until I tasted the loaf baked every day at Nick Nairn's Cook School at Port of Monteith: it is light, airy – and with a terrific crust, something I had not been successful with before. But then I investigated the use of dried milk or milk powder, which is invariably advocated by makers of bread machines. The reason is twofold: it enables you to add more liquid and it also produces a softer texture of crumb and a softer crust. Now, maybe bread-machine manufacturers imagine we Brits prefer pappy crusts that are easily gummed when we remove our dentures, but I for one do not. And so, leave out the dried milk if you want a decent crust. If, however, you do want a soft crust, add one tablespoon dried milk into the basic White Loaf mix below. It is also important to remove the loaf immediately the programme is finished, otherwise it will steam and you will lose your crispy crust.

The following recipes work for me. Your machine might have different programme settings, in which case adjust accordingly.

White loaf

MAKES 1 LOAF

1 teaspoon fast-action/easy-blend dried yeast	1½ teaspoons salt
550g/1 lb 4 oz/4¾ cups unbleached strong white flour	1 tablespoon golden granulated sugar
	25g/1 oz/¼ stick unsalted butter, diced

1 Sprinkle the yeast over the base of the pan. Add the flour and level off. Sprinkle over the salt then the sugar, and then add the butter, ensuring they are well distributed.

2 Add 300ml/½ pint/1⅓ cups cold water then set to bake for a Basic Loaf with a Dark Crust (my machine takes 3 hours 13 minutes for this). Avoid Rapid Bakes if possible.

Nairn's cook school loaf

This is my adaptation of Nick Nairn's famous loaf and is my favourite.

MAKES 1 LOAF

2 teaspoons golden granulated sugar

2 teaspoons salt

2 tablespoons extra virgin olive oil

570g/1 lb 4$\frac{1}{2}$ oz/5 cups unbleached strong white flour

7g/$\frac{1}{4}$ oz sachet of fast-action/easy-blend dried yeast

1 Sprinkle the sugar then the salt into the pan, and then drizzle in the oil. Add 350ml/ 12 fl oz/1$\frac{1}{2}$ cups cold water then the flour, levelling the surface gently. Finally, sprinkle over the yeast.

2 Set to bake for a Basic Loaf with a Dark Crust (my machine takes 3 hours 13 minutes).

Wholemeal loaf

MAKES 1 LOAF

1$\frac{1}{2}$ teaspoons fast-action/easy-blend dried yeast

300g/10$\frac{1}{2}$ oz/2$\frac{1}{2}$ cups strong wholemeal flour

250g/9 oz/2 cups strong white unbleached flour

2 teaspoons golden caster sugar

1$\frac{1}{2}$ teaspoons salt

25g/1 oz/$\frac{1}{4}$ stick unsalted butter, diced

1 Place the yeast in the pan, and then the flours. Sprinkle over the sugar and salt, and then dot over the butter.

2 Pour in 350ml/12 fl oz/1$\frac{1}{2}$ cups cold water and set for a Wholemeal Loaf with a Dark Crust (my machine takes 3 hours 43 minutes).

BREAD TIPS

1 Unbleached flour gives far more character to a loaf.

2 Ensure you have enough salt in your dough otherwise it will be tasteless.

3 Fast-action or easy-blend dried yeast is my preferred option as it is always to hand, but if you use fresh yeast, use 15g/^{1}/$_2$ oz (dissolved in some of the tepid liquid with ^{1}/$_2$ teaspoon sugar and left to stand for 10 minutes). This mixture is then added with the remaining tepid liquid.

4 In order to achieve the perfect temperature for tepid or 'hand-hot' liquid, mix one-third boiling liquid to two-thirds cold; it should feel pleasantly and comfortably warm.

5 You can replace some of the tepid water with tepid milk if you want less of a chewy texture and more of a soft crumb.

6 The easiest way to incorporate liquids into dry ingredients is to make a well in the centre of the dry ingredients and gradually pour in the liquids with one hand while drawing in the flour with a spoon held in the other hand.

7 The wetter the dough, the better the bread, so add enough to make a fairly soft, but not too sticky, dough. However, if you add too much liquid it will be impossible to knead.

8 Kneading by hand is my preferred method (the best stress-reliever!) but you can also knead in a free-standing mixer, such as a KitchenAid, using a dough hook.

9 To knead by hand, stretch the dough away from you with the heel of your hand then turn the dough and repeat the movement. Ten minutes is usually enough for the texture to change and become smoother and more elastic.

10 The ideal temperature for bread dough to rise is 20–25°C/68–77°F, which is the temperature of most airing cupboards, but you can leave it in the refrigerator overnight or at room temperature for an hour or so longer. Never leave it somewhere hot, such as on top of a radiator. Ensure your bowl is tightly covered so that it is draught-free. Regular doughs will take anything from 1–2 hours (my house is cold and so I always allow 2) but enriched doughs take an hour or so longer. Slowly risen dough has a better taste and texture.

11 Leaving a dough to rise overnight in the refrigerator is perfect if you have guests the next day so you can achieve the homely bread-baking aromas but you have done the hard work of measuring and kneading the day before. This method also ensures a truly flavoursome loaf after a slow rising. Simply cover the bowl of kneaded dough and place in the refrigerator for at least 12 hours. Next day remove to room temperature (the dough will be harder than usual), knock back and shape as usual but give the second rising longer – I usually leave it for up to an hour.

12 To knock back or punch down dough means to punch a risen dough to deflate the air bubbles; this takes place after the first rising.

13 To shape bread, form into a round loaf, or long baguette shape or oval, or shape into rolls. Tuck any edges underneath. I always prefer a 'free-form' loaf to one packed into a tin as it has more crust (and looks more home-made!).

14 Loaves can be glazed: brush with beaten egg, or beaten egg yolk or milk before baking; with olive oil or melted butter immediately after baking. You can also simply dust with flour, fine oatmeal or fine polenta prior to baking if you prefer a less shiny crust.

15 Bread is usually baked at a very high oven temperature (although enriched doughs are usually a little lower) but chef Sally Clarke's method is also excellent if you are worried about heating your oven to its highest temperature: you place the bread in a medium heat which gets the insides cooking then immediately increase to high. This method ensures that a crust does not form at once thereby inhibiting the insides cooking through. Most commercial loaves – and pizzas – are baked at a minimum temperature of 230°C/450°F/Gas 8, which many domestic ovens simply cannot reach, so Sally's method is ideal if you are nervous about very high oven temperatures.

16 To test whether bread is cooked, remove the loaf and turn upside down, wearing oven gloves, then tap the loaf underneath: if it is ready it will sound hollow, like a drum; if it is heavy or dense return to the oven for a few more minutes.

17 Tempting though it may be, only cut loaves when they are cold or they will become soggy.

Classic   Bread-machine   Aga

SODA BREAD

Based on traditional Irish soda bread, this recipe uses a mixture of wholemeal and plain flour, for a good texture and flavour but without being too heavy going. I sometimes add a couple of tablespoons of pinhead oatmeal for an even nuttier texture, adding a little more liquid accordingly. Buttermilk is now easy to find in supermarkets and is ideal for soda bread. The alkali (bicarbonate of soda) combined with the acidic buttermilk (or sour milk, used in the past before refrigerators were commonplace) produces an immediate reaction. The acid in the buttermilk helps aeration, producing a light texture. If you cannot find buttermilk, use sour cream diluted with enough water to give a pouring consistency.

An Irish friend who has made soda bread all her life said the trick is not to knead as such, but simply to pat into shape. She 'kneads' the dough only until the underside of the dough is smooth. If you think 'light touch' and scone-making instead of 'energetic kneading' and bread-making, your soda bread will be perfect.

MAKES 1 LOAF

300g/10$\frac{1}{2}$ oz/2$\frac{1}{2}$ cups plain wholemeal flour
150g/5$\frac{1}{2}$ oz/1$\frac{1}{4}$ cups plain flour, sifted
1 teaspoon bicarbonate of soda
1 teaspoon sugar

1 teaspoon salt
300ml/10 fl oz/1$\frac{1}{3}$ cups buttermilk
about 100ml/3$\frac{1}{2}$ fl oz/$\frac{1}{2}$ cup milk

1 Preheat the oven to 230°C/450°F/Gas 8. Place the flours, bicarbonate of soda, sugar and salt in a bowl and mix.

2 Make a well in the centre. Slowly pour in the buttermilk and milk, while drawing the flour into the liquid in the middle. Combine to form a fairly soft but not sticky dough, adding more milk if necessary. Bring it together with your hands and turn out on to a floured surface. Knead gently for a couple of seconds (this should be more patting out than vigorous kneading), just enough to shape the dough into a round, about 6cm/2$\frac{1}{2}$ in deep. Lightly oil a baking sheet. Place the dough on the baking sheet and slash a shallow cross across the top.

3 Bake for 15 minutes then reduce the temperature to 200°C/400°F/Gas 6 and continue to bake for a further 25 minutes or until the loaf, once tapped underneath, sounds hollow. Remove to a wire rack and cool before cutting and spreading with butter.

HAGGIS BREAD

This is an unusual but extremely delicious bread and is great either fresh or toasted after a couple of days – and served with a smear of butter and a sliver of farmhouse cheese . . . Scottish of course.

The idea is from butcher Lindsay Grieve in Hawick: best known for his award-winning haggis, but the idea to incorporate haggis into a loaf of bread came while he was watching Jamie Oliver throw everything from cheese and Parma ham to herbs, courgettes and nuts into a basic bread dough. I have stolen (with the butcher's permission!) the concept and made it into this very tasty loaf. You will need only a small amount of haggis for this so use the rest in stuffing for roast chicken – or spoon into little tartlets with a red onion marmalade on top and serve with drinks.

MAKES 1 LOAF

700g/1 lb 9 oz/6 cups unbleached strong bread flour (I mix white and wholemeal)

7g/¼ oz sachet of fast-action/easy-blend dried yeast

2 teaspoons salt

100g/3½ oz cold haggis, crumbled loosely

fine or medium oatmeal, to sprinkle

1 Combine the flour, yeast and salt in a bowl. Make a well in the centre then stir in the haggis and enough tepid water (425–450ml/15–16 fl oz/1²/₃ –2 cups) to make a fairly soft dough that will come together with your hands.

2 Turn on to a lightly floured surface and knead for 10 minutes until smooth. Place in a lightly oiled bowl and cover with clingfilm. Leave in a warm place for 1½–2 hours until well risen, then knock back and shape into a haggis-shaped loaf. Lightly oil a baking sheet. Place the dough on the baking sheet, cover loosely with oiled clingfilm, then leave to rise in a warm place for about 45 minutes. Meanwhile, preheat the oven to 230°C/450°F/Gas 8.

3 Sprinkle some oatmeal over the dough and bake for 15 minutes, then turn the temperature down to 200°C/400°F/Gas 6. Continue to bake for a further 25 minutes or so, until done: test by tapping the underneath – it should sound hollow. Remove to a wire rack to cool completely.

DUKKAH BREAD

As a guest of Tasting Australia in Adelaide, I toured the food and wine festival to find many delights, one of which was *dukkah* (pronounced doo-kah) bread. *Dukkah* is an Egyptian spice mix, usually eaten in Egypt with bread dipped in olive oil – for breakfast or as an appetiser. It is classically a mixture of roasted sesame seeds, cumin and coriander mixed with roasted and crushed hazelnuts, but in South Australia macadamia nuts are often used instead. *Dukkah* is now commercially available but if you cannot find it, here is a simple recipe.

FOR THE *DUKKAH*
75g/2³/₄ oz/¹/₂ cup sesame seeds
25g/1 oz/¹/₂ cup cumin seeds
25g/1 oz/³/₄ cup coriander seeds
50g/1³/₄ oz/¹/₂ cup hazelnuts or macadamia
    nuts, roughly chopped
salt and freshly ground pepper

FOR THE BREAD
700g/1 lb 9 oz/6 cups unbleached strong bread
    flour (I mix white and wholemeal)
7g/¹/₄ oz sachet of fast-action/easy-blend
    dried yeast
2 teaspoons salt

1 To make the *dukkah*, roast the seeds and nuts until toasted and a spicy aroma arises: either under the grill for 1–2 minutes or in a heavy frying pan without fat for 3–5 minutes, shaking the pan often. Place in a small electric blender or spice mill and blitz briefly (using the pulse button) until the spices are crushed but still dry – not oily – then add salt and pepper to taste.

2 To make the bread, combine the flour, yeast and salt in a bowl. Make a well in the centre then stir in 75g/2³/₄ oz/1 cup of the *dukkah* and enough tepid water (425–450ml/ 15–16 fl oz/1²/₃–2 cups) to make a fairly soft dough that will come together with your hands.

3 Turn on to a lightly floured surface and knead for 10 minutes until smooth. Place in a lightly oiled bowl and cover with clingfilm. Leave in a warm place for 1¹/₂–2 hours until well risen, then knock back and shape into a loaf. Lightly oil a baking sheet. Place the dough on the baking sheet, cover loosely with oiled clingfilm, then leave to rise in a warm place for about 45 minutes. Meanwhile, preheat the oven to 230°C/450°F/Gas 8.

4 Bake for 15 minutes, then turn the temperature down to 200°C/400°F/Gas 6. Continue to bake for a further 25 minutes or so, until done: test by tapping the underneath – it should sound hollow. Remove to a wire rack to cool completely.

OLIVE OIL LOAVES

It is easy to make this tasty, moist bread – similar to ciabatta – which is also rather a messy dough to handle, as it is rather loose and almost batter-like. The trick for making this bread is to flour your hands lightly (and I reiterate the word lightly) and the board often – and also to work as quickly as possible.

I like to use mainly 00 flour for Italian loaves including ciabatta as, although most loaves and pizzas are made with 0 flour (which is higher in gluten) in Italy, this is not readily available in the UK and so 00 flour is good, as a soft texture is required. According to Anna Del Conte, Italian flour is milled differently from British flour and the gluten ground less finely, which means that when bread is baked it retains more water, thus producing a softer and lighter crumb.

Although flavourings for this loaf, such as herbs, tomatoes and red onions, are entirely optional, I offer a variation that is utterly delicious, if a little unusual both in taste and appearance. It is squid ink bread, based on an excellent loaf I enjoyed at the Palazzo Sasso in Ravello on the Amalfi coast. There the black bread is served either as a sandwich of octopus and cherry tomatoes or with whiter-than-white local buffalo mozzarella and tomato in a salad. The bright vivid colours of these would put Gauguin to shame. To make the squid ink bread pour two 4g/^{1}/$_8$ oz sachets of squid ink into the well with the oil and water and combine thoroughly. Proceed as normal. Your hands and the board will become completely black, but it washes off easily.

MAKES 2 LOAVES

450g/1 lb/4 cups Italian 00 flour
200g/7 oz/1^3/$_4$ cups unbleached strong
   white flour

7g/^{1}/$_4$ oz sachet of fast-action/easy-blend
   dried yeast
2 teaspoons salt
6 tablespoons olive oil

1 Place both flours, the yeast and salt in a bowl, stir together then make a well in the centre.

2 Pour in the oil and 450ml/16 fl oz/2 cups tepid water and combine together with a spoon. Using floured hands, bring together and knead briskly for 10 minutes or until smooth, then place in a bowl and cover with oiled clingfilm. Leave somewhere warm for about 1½ hours until risen.

3 Lightly oil a baking sheet. Divide the dough into two and shape loosely into two long ovals. Place on the baking sheet and cover loosely with oiled clingfilm. Leave for 45 minutes. Meanwhile, preheat the oven to 220°C/425°F/Gas 7. Bake for 30 minutes or until the loaves sound hollow when tapped underneath. Cool on a wire rack.

FOCACCIA STUFFED WITH TALEGGIO AND HAM

This focaccia differs from the classic Ligurian bread topped with local olive oil and strewn with sea salt. It is stuffed with ham and cheese that melts as it bakes; a kind of sophisticated cheese-and-ham toastie. And I can assure you, it wins hands down on taste.

SERVES 6–8

500g/1 lb 2 oz/4$\frac{1}{3}$ cups Italian 00 flour

7g/$\frac{1}{4}$ oz sachet of fast-action/easy-blend dried yeast

1 heaped teaspoon salt

3 tablespoons extra virgin olive oil

100g/3$\frac{1}{2}$ oz good quality cooked ham

150g/5$\frac{1}{2}$ oz cubed Taleggio cheese, rind removed

40g/1$\frac{1}{2}$ oz (a handful) rocket

1 Make the bread dough by mixing the flour, yeast and salt in a large bowl. Mix the oil with 275ml/9$\frac{1}{2}$ fl oz/1$\frac{1}{4}$ cups tepid water and pour into the flour, adding a touch more tepid water if necessary; you should have a fairly soft dough that comes away from the sides of the bowl.

2 Tip this on to a floured surface and knead for 10 minutes, until smooth. Place the dough in an oiled bowl, cover with clingfilm and place somewhere fairly warm to rise for 1$\frac{1}{2}$–2 hours. Divide into two pieces and roll each out to fit a 23 × 33cm/9 × 13 in Swiss roll tin.

3 Place one piece in the tin, top with the ham, cheese and rocket (strewing everything casually over), then cover with the other piece, crimping the edges to seal. Cover and leave for 30 minutes. Meanwhile, preheat the oven to 220°C/425°F /Gas 7. Brush the focaccia with olive oil, prick it all over with a fork and bake for 20–25 minutes until golden brown. Cut into large sections and eat warm while the cheese is still gooey.

STOTTIE CAKES

Newcastle's answer to the focaccia, stottie cake is every bit as tasty and is traditionally made in the same way – on the bottom of a coal-fired oven. Both 'hearth' breads would have been baked with leftover dough from the regular loaves and baked either directly on the oven floor or on a flat baking tray. Stottie cakes are hugely popular in the north-east of England where they are often served split and filled with ham and pease pudding – or even butter and jam for tea. But I also like them split and filled with more Mediterranean fillings such as roasted vegetables, salami and rocket or tomatoes, mozzarella and basil leaves – all drizzled with a little olive oil.

Why are we not buying stottie sandwiches in every sandwich bar in the land instead of the ubiquitous focaccia, delicious though it is? I somehow cannot imagine stotties being all the rage down in Genoa.

MAKES 2

500g/1 lb 2 oz/4$\frac{1}{3}$ cups unbleached strong white flour

1 heaped teaspoon salt

7g/$\frac{1}{4}$ oz sachet of fast-action/easy-blend dried yeast

25g/1 oz/$\frac{1}{4}$ stick unsalted butter, diced

1 Mix the flour, salt and yeast in a bowl, then rub in the butter until it resembles breadcrumbs.

2 Slowly add about 300ml/$\frac{1}{2}$ pint/1$\frac{1}{3}$ cups tepid water and bring together to form a dough. Turn on to a floured surface and knead for up to 10 minutes until smooth. Place in a bowl and cover with clingfilm. Leave in a warm place for about 1 hour or until well risen.

3 Lightly oil a baking sheet. Knock back the dough and divide into two pieces. Shape each piece by gently pushing the dough into a disc, about 23cm/9 in diameter. Place on the baking sheet and leave to rise in a warm place for about 20 minutes. Meanwhile, preheat the oven to 220°C/425°F /Gas 7.

4 Create a series of dimples over the top of each cake by pressing with your fingers. Bake for 10 minutes then turn the cake over. Bake for a further 4–5 minutes or until golden brown on top and cooked through. Cool on a wire rack before slicing in two.

WHOLEMEAL WALNUT LOAF

Warning: this loaf is good for you! Based on the famous Grant loaf, it is a seriously healthy loaf that is delicious either thinly sliced and served freshly made, or thickly sliced and toasted. I like it buttered and served with a tangy farmhouse goat's milk cheese.

And look at the recipe – there is no kneading required at all. According to Doris Grant in her 1961 book *Your Bread & Your Life* it is the 'no kneading' that accounts for the loaf's delicious flavour. She says that the air spaces formed by the yeast working in the dough may contain some undiscovered vitamins or other qualities in stoneground wholewheat flour. When these air spaces are broken during kneading, these qualities escape and are lost. Her theory was confirmed by an experienced baker who agreed that wholewheat bread must never be kneaded and told her that it did not matter two hoots if white bread was kneaded or not, as it had already lost most of its goodness in the milling process.

After she first published her recipe in 1944, Mrs Grant had endless correspondence on how her bread had changed people's lives, since the use of wholewheat flour was essential for a healthy diet; her conviction was also a reaction against the ubiquity of cheap, processed flours heavily treated with chemicals. When she was speaking in Tyneside, a miner told her how different his health had become since his wife had begun baking the Grant loaf daily. She also illustrated the health-giving properties of wholewheat flour by writing that the Channel Islanders were much healthier during the German Occupation in the Second World War because the bakers had to use wholegrain German flour instead of processed white British flour.

Besides the fact that this wholemeal bread is healthy, it is also a moist, tasty loaf and is ridiculously easy to make. It is the perfect example of Escoffier's famous adage '*Faites simple*', which can only be done to effect with the best and most natural ingredients.

MAKES 1 LOAF

650g/1 lb 7 oz/5$^{1}/_{2}$ cups strong wholemeal flour

7g/$^{1}/_{4}$ oz sachet of fast-action/easy-blend dried yeast

2 teaspoons salt

100g/3$^{1}/_{2}$ oz/$^{3}/_{4}$ cup walnuts, chopped

1 Mix the flour in a large bowl with the yeast and salt. Slowly pour in 550ml/19 fl oz/2$^{1}/_{2}$ cups tepid water and the walnuts, stirring all the time with a wooden spoon. Stir for 2–3 minutes, working from the sides into middle, until the dough leaves the sides of the mixing bowl clean.

2 Butter a 900g/2 lb loaf tin well (it is a heavier dough so butter the tins well or it may stick to the sides). Place the dough in the tin. Cover loosely with oiled clingfilm and leave in a warm place for 45–60 minutes until it has risen. Meanwhile, preheat the oven to 230°C/450°F/Gas 8.

3 Bake for 40–45 minutes or until the loaf sounds hollow when tapped underneath. Cover loosely with foil for the last 10 minutes if it looks too brown. Remove to a wire rack to cool.

FLATBREADS

This is a basic flatbread recipe that can be adapted depending on which sort of dish you want to use it for. The three methods given here – oven, frying pan and barbecue – make completely different types of bread, albeit from the same batch of dough. The oven bread is softer and puffier, more naan bread or pitta-like. The frying pan and barbecued bread is flatter and becomes more charred and scorched because the heat is more direct – giving a more Middle-eastern, Turkish-style bread. Whichever you decide to make, be sure to wrap them in a tea cloth to keep them warm and soft while you make the entire batch.

MAKES 6

250g/9 oz/2 cups unbleached strong white flour

1 teaspoon fast-action/easy-blend dried yeast
¾ teaspoon salt

1 Put the flour, yeast and salt in a bowl and mix together. Slowly pour in enough tepid water (175–200ml/6–7 fl oz/¾ cup) to form a fairly soft dough that you can combine in your (lightly floured) hands into a ball. Knead for 5 minutes on a floured surface until smooth then place in a bowl and cover with clingfilm. Leave somewhere warm for about an hour until risen.

2 Divide the dough into six pieces and roll each out on a floured surface to 15–20cm/6–8 in. Cover each one with a cloth while you roll out the others.

3 To cook in the oven: preheat the oven to 230°C/450°F/Gas 8 and put a baking sheet inside to heat. Place a couple of flatbreads on the hot baking sheet at the top of the oven and bake for 5–7 minutes, until puffed up in parts and cooked yet still pliable.

4 To cook in a pan: heat a heavy-based frying pan or a flat griddle pan to very hot (this will take some time), then place a flatbread in the pan (without adding fat) and cook for 2 minutes. Turn and, pressing down to deflate any air bubbles, cook on the other side until done. This will take 1–2 minutes. Stack the flatbreads and cover with a cloth while you cook the remainder.

5 To cook on a barbecue: leave the rolled-out dough on a board for about 10 minutes. Brush the tops with sunflower or olive oil, slap on to a hot barbecue, oil-side down and lightly brush the top side with oil. Sprinkle over some flakes of sea salt. Cook for 1–2 minutes each side, until puffed up and patched with golden brown.

CHAPATIS

Eat warm with all sorts of Indian-style dishes.

MAKES 4

200g/7 oz/1¾ cups plain wholemeal flour
good pinch of salt

1 tablespoon sunflower oil, plus extra
for greasing

1 Sift the flour and salt into a bowl, then stir in the sunflower oil. Add just enough warm water (about 150ml/5 fl oz/⅔ cup) to form a firm dough, then gather the dough together with your hands and knead for about 8–10 minutes until smooth.

2 Place in a bowl, cover with a damp cloth and leave at room temperature for at least 30 minutes. Divide into four, then roll each piece on a lightly floured surface to a thin circle 15cm/6 in diameter.

3 Heat a griddle or large, solid frying pan to hot, and preheat the grill to hot. Oil the pan very lightly, then slap on the chapati and cook on one side for 1–1½ minutes, before turning and cooking for another 1 minute. Place under the grill for ½–1 minute until puffed up in irregular bulges and scorched, watching carefully as it can burn easily. (The more traditional way to finish them off is over a direct flame: using oven gloves and two pairs of tongs, hold the chapati over a direct flame, for about 20 seconds on each side, or until it puffs up). Repeat with the remaining three chapatis.

4 Keep them stacked together under a large napkin or cloth until serving time and eat warm.

CORNBREAD

I first encountered American cornbread in Santa Fe, where it is served in restaurant bread baskets alongside the French stick. And although I love the almost scone-like texture and usually fiery flavourings, I dislike many cornbreads in the United States as they are so terribly sweet. They are, after all, meant to be served with stews, chillies and baked beans. So I have reduced the amount of sugar considerably; the effect is the same cakey texture but with a more savoury taste. Although cornmeal is authentic, polenta will work perfectly well for this if it is more easily available. Use one of the three alternative flavourings I have suggested below.

SERVES 8–10

200g/7 oz/1¾ cups plain flour

2 teaspoons baking powder

1 teaspoon salt

140g/5 oz/1 cup cornmeal or polenta

20g/¾ oz/1½ tablespoons golden
    caster sugar

150ml/5 fl oz/⅔ cup milk

1 large free-range egg

40g/1½ oz/½ stick unsalted butter, melted

FOR THE FLAVOURINGS

1 tablespoon chopped green chillies and
    1 tablespoon freshly chopped coriander

or 2 tablespoons sweetcorn and 1 teaspoon
    ground cumin and 1 teaspoon finely
    chopped red chilli

or 1 heaped tablespoon freshly chopped
    oregano and 2 tablespoons grated mature
    Cheddar cheese

1 Butter an 18cm/7 in square baking tin and preheat the oven to 190°C/375°F/Gas 5. Sift the flour and baking powder into a bowl with the salt and the cornmeal or polenta. Stir in the sugar, then add your choice of flavouring.

2 In a separate bowl mix the milk, egg and butter, then tip into the mixture. Gently combine as quickly as possible, then tip into the prepared tin. Bake for 25–30 minutes until tinged with golden brown and a skewer inserted to the middle comes out clean.

3 Leave in the tin for 5 minutes or so then cut into squares and place on a wire rack to cool.

STICKY CARDAMOM AND CINNAMON BUNS

These Finnish buns called *pulla* are as commonplace to Finns as scones are to us. It is basically a cardamom-flavoured sweet bread (cardamom is a typical and everyday spice, having been imported into Finland for both medicinal and culinary use since the sixteenth century) and is served with coffee – or when freshly baked and still warm, with a long glass of ice-cold milk.

The basic recipe is used in many ways, such as this one – *korvapuustit*. The dough can also be stretched into a Swiss roll tin, topped with lingonberries or blueberries and baked as a berry pie – *Isoaidin pulla* or Grandmother's *pulla*.

I absolutely adore these buns as, not only do they take me back to my year in the north of Finland where these were made by every household I visited, but they also taste divine.

MAKES 20

500g/1 lb 2 oz/4$\frac{1}{3}$ cups strong white flour
25g/1 oz/2 tablespoons golden caster sugar
7g/$\frac{1}{4}$ oz sachet of fast-action/easy-blend
   dried yeast
1 teaspoon salt
85g/3 oz/$\frac{3}{4}$ stick unsalted butter, diced
2 teaspoons crushed cardamom seeds (remove
   black seeds from green pods and crush)
300ml/$\frac{1}{2}$ pint/1$\frac{1}{3}$ cups tepid milk

FOR THE FILLING
70g/2$\frac{1}{2}$ oz/$\frac{3}{4}$ stick unsalted butter, softened
70g/2$\frac{1}{2}$ oz/$\frac{1}{3}$ cup light muscovado sugar
2 teaspoons ground cinnamon
1 medium free-range egg, beaten, to glaze

1 Place the flour, sugar, yeast and salt in a bowl and combine well. Rub in the butter and stir in the crushed cardamom seeds. Make a well in the centre, then pour in the milk, bringing the mixture together with a spoon. Combine with your hands to form a dough.

2 Turn on to a floured surface and knead for 10 minutes or until smooth. Place in a lightly oiled bowl, cover with clingfilm and leave to rise in a warm place for 2–3 hours. Meanwhile, put 20 paper cases on a baking sheet.

3 Knock back the dough, and gently roll with a rolling pin or press out gently with the heels of your hands to make a 28 × 38cm/11 × 15 in rectangle. Spread with the softened butter for the filling, and sprinkle over the sugar and cinnamon.

4 Roll up, Swiss roll style, along the long side to make a roly-poly. Cut into 20 slices. Place these, cut-side up, in the paper cases close together. Cover loosely with clingfilm and leave to rise for 30–40 minutes. Meanwhile, preheat the oven to 220°C/425°F/Gas 7.

5 Gently press down on the centre of each bun, using your index finger, so that the spiral-like filling bulges upwards. Brush with beaten egg and bake for about 10 minutes or until golden brown. Transfer to a wire rack to cool. Eat warm, preferably with a glass of cold milk.

CHELSEA BUNS

These buns were made famous during the eighteenth century at The Chelsea Bun House, situated in the Borough of Chelsea, where there were long queues of people waiting to buy the prized – and hugely popular – sticky buns. Chelsea buns look stunning – and are not at all difficult to make. Although the original recipe does not contain cinnamon, I think the fragrant, warm taste of cinnamon enhances what has to be one of the best – and most British – of buns.

MAKES 9

450g/1 lb/4 cups strong white bread flour

2 teaspoons ground cinnamon

$\frac{1}{2}$ teaspoon salt

50g/1$\frac{3}{4}$ oz/$\frac{1}{2}$ stick unsalted butter, cubed

7g/$\frac{1}{4}$ oz sachet fast-action/easy-blend dried yeast

25g/1 oz/2 tablespoons golden caster sugar

1 medium free-range egg

225–250ml/8–9 fl oz/1 cup lukewarm milk

FOR THE TOPPING

40g/1$\frac{1}{2}$ oz/$\frac{1}{2}$ stick unsalted butter, melted

50g/1$\frac{3}{4}$ oz/$\frac{1}{3}$ cup each raisins, currants and sultanas

50g/1$\frac{3}{4}$ oz/$\frac{1}{4}$ cup light muscovado sugar

2 teaspoons clear honey

1 Sift the flour, cinnamon and salt into a large bowl. Rub in the butter until it resembles breadcrumbs, then stir in the yeast, combining well.

2 In another bowl, whisk together the caster sugar and egg. Pour in 225ml/8 fl oz/1 cup of the lukewarm milk. Add this liquid to the dry ingredients and, using a spoon, mix to a dough in the bowl. (Add a splash more tepid milk if necessary.)

3 Turn the dough on to a lightly floured surface and knead for about 10 minutes, until the dough feels smooth. Place in a lightly oiled bowl, cover with oiled clingfilm and leave in a warm place for 2–3 hours until almost doubled in size. Alternatively, leave it overnight in the refrigerator (allow it to return to room temperature the next day before using).

4 Butter a 23cm/9 in square tin. Remove the clingfilm and tip out the dough on to a lightly floured surface. Gently roll it out into a rectangle, about 25 × 35cm/10 × 14 in, or press into shape with the heels of your hands.

5 To make the topping, melt the butter and brush it all over the dough. Mix the dried fruits together with the sugar and sprinkle evenly over the butter, leaving a 1cm/½ in border all around.

6 Place both hands at the long side of the rectangle (the side farthest away from you) and very carefully roll up the dough towards you, as if you are rolling a Swiss roll. (Poke any wayward fruit back in.) Press the joins gently together to seal.

7 Using a sharp knife, cut the roll into nine even pieces. Arrange the pieces, cut side up, so that you can see the pinwheels of fruit. The pieces should be just touching. Warm 1 teaspoon honey (I do this by placing a small dish of honey in the microwave for a couple of turns; alternatively, place the jar in a pan of very hot water). Brush the honey over the buns, then cover loosely with oiled clingfilm. Leave them to rise in a warm place for about 30–45 minutes, until they have risen and look slightly puffy. Meanwhile, preheat the oven to 200°C/400°F/Gas 6.

8 Remove the clingfilm and place the buns in the middle of the oven. Bake for about 25 minutes, or until golden brown. Remove and brush with the remaining warm honey.

9 Leave them in the tin for 2–3 minutes, and then carefully remove them to a wire rack to cool. (Rather than tipping them out, which means that some fruit will fall out, try to lever them out using two large fish slices.) Pull the buns apart only once they have cooled for at least 10 minutes – if you can wait that long!

RAISIN AND ROSEMARY LOAF

This is a flavoursome and moist loaf that is good to eat fresh, but also toasts really well; eaten fresh I cut it fairly thinly but when toasted I like it nice and thick. Serve with a sharp cheese such as a farmhouse sheep's milk cheese – perhaps with some grapes and nuts – and you have the most satisfying lunch or final course to supper. You will also have a sudden urge to open yet another bottle of gutsy red to accompany it. Yield to temptation just this once.

MAKES 1 LOAF

450g/1 lb/4 cups unbleached strong white
  flour, sifted
200g/7 oz/1¾ cups unbleached strong
  wholemeal flour
2 teaspoons salt

7g/¼ oz sachet of fast-action/easy-blend
  dried yeast
2 tablespoons, plus 1 teaspoon, clear honey
2 tablespoons olive oil
140g/5 oz/1 cup raisins
1 tablespoon young rosemary, finely chopped

1 Place the flours in a bowl with the salt and yeast. Stir together.

2 Make a well in the centre and pour in the 2 tablespoons honey and the oil, then add about 350ml/12 fl oz/1½ cups tepid water – enough to combine to a fairly firm dough. Add the raisins and rosemary and combine with your hands. Tip on to a floured surface and knead for about 10 minutes or until smooth.

3 Place in a lightly oiled bowl and cover with clingfilm, then leave in a warm place for 1½–2 hours or until well risen. Oil a 900g/2 lb loaf tin. Knock back the dough and shape into a loaf, tucking the ends underneath. Place in the loaf tin, gently easing the dough into shape. Loosely cover with oiled clingfilm and leave in a warm place for at least 45 minutes or until well risen; it should rise above the lip of the tin. Meanwhile, preheat the oven to 230°C/450°F/Gas 8.

4 Melt the 1 teaspoon honey (I do this in the microwave for a few seconds) and brush over the top of the loaf, taking care not to brush the side of the tin or the loaf will stick. Place in the oven for 15 minutes, then reduce the temperature to 200°C/400°F/Gas 6. Cover the bread loosely with foil, then continue to bake for a further 20–25 minutes or until the loaf, once tapped underneath, sounds hollow. Cool completely on a wire rack before slicing.

BRIOCHE

I have not only been unsuccessful with brioches in the past, I have always been put off by the ridiculously lengthy instructions for making them. But one look at the short, sensible recipe by Australian chef Maggie Beer in her brilliant book *Maggie's Table* and I was ready to try again. Maggie says the most important thing about brioche is giving it time to rise. She also has a recipe for an olive oil brioche made with a fruity olive oil instead of butter. And both doughs are put in the refrigerator out of the heat of the kitchen. Since the climate of South Australia is just a little different from ours in Britain, I recommend the normal 'warm place' – but leave for a longer time than you would with regular bread dough. Follow these instructions and your brioche will be lightly textured with a fabulously buttery taste that cries out for either a smear of butter and home-made jam for breakfast or a slice of duck liver pâté for lunch.

MAKES 1

500g/1 lb 2 oz/4⅓ cups unbleached strong white flour

7g/¼ oz sachet of fast-action/easy-blend dried yeast

25g/1 oz/2 tablespoons golden caster sugar

1 teaspoon salt

200g/7 oz/2 sticks unsalted butter, melted and cooled for 2–3 minutes

50ml/2 fl oz/¼ cup milk

4 large free-range eggs, beaten

1 medium free-range egg, to glaze (optional)

1 Place the flour, yeast, sugar and salt in a food mixer and combine briefly with the dough hook (this recipe is too sloppy to do by hand). In a separate bowl whisk together the melted butter, milk and eggs (this mixture is tepid, because of the butter). Slowly add to the flour mixture with the machine running. Continue to knead in the machine for 5 minutes, then remove the bowl and hook. Cover the bowl and leave in a warm place for 3–4 hours until risen.

2 Butter a deep 18cm/7 in cake tin or brioche mould. Return the bowl to the machine, replace the dough hook and knead again in the machine for 5 minutes. If using a cake tin, simply place the dough inside, ensuring it is more or less even on top. If using a mould, put two-thirds of it inside and shape the remaining dough into a ball, place it on top and press gently down.

3 Cover loosely with oiled clingfilm and leave for another 3–4 hours, or until the dough has reached the top of the tin. Meanwhile, preheat the oven to 220°C/425°F/Gas 7. If you are glazing, do so now, ensuring the egg does not spill down the sides of the tin. (I don't bother to glaze, as the resulting crust is wonderfully golden brown anyway; but for the ultimate sheen, glaze!)

4 Bake for 20 minutes then turn the temperature down to 190°C/375°F/Gas 5 and continue to bake for a further 20 minutes, covering loosely with foil after 10 minutes, until well risen and golden brown. Turn out on to a wire rack to cool completely before cutting.

Savoury pies, pastries and tarts

I have always loved pies and savoury pastries, ever since that classic of my childhood, bacon and egg pie, was transformed as if by magic into the 1970s classic, quiche Lorraine (without much alteration in many cases). I often used to enjoy Scotch pies or Forfar bridies, their perfectly crusty (never hard) outers containing the warm, meaty, gravy-moistened inners. I have since happily rolled out many a pastry case before filling then baking and allowing to cool for just long enough, before scoffing with indecent haste. And although puff pastry is handy to buy and there are some excellent all-butter ones available now, and good filo pastry is also widely available, I usually prefer good home-made shortcrust pastry. It can be enhanced by the addition of grated cheese, oatmeal, herbs or polenta, and fillings can include meat, fish, vegetables or cheese. Savoury pies and tarts are incredibly versatile, suitable for any time of day and for any meal. What, have you never sneaked a cold slab of last night's quiche for breakfast?

TOMATO AND TAPENADE TART

This looks good and tastes good, topped with either some slices of yummy black pudding or an inviting little heap of rocket. The rocket topping is one that you know everyone will like, but for those black-pudding eaters out there, this one is for you. As I adore black pudding in a soft bap or ciabatta roll with a smear of tapenade and a slice of tomato, I thought it might convert into a tart nicely; in my opinion it does.

One of my favourites is Stornoway black pudding (from Charles Macleod on the Isle of Lewis), which is nicely firm and has a true flavour and crunchy texture. Another one I love, but that has a far softer texture, is Macsween's black pudding, which has an almost melting texture and rich flavour that has been described as 'chocolate-cakey'. You just have to try it and see.

SERVES 8

175g/6 oz/1½ cups plain flour, sifted
25g/1 oz/2 tablespoons fine or medium
   oatmeal
115g/4 oz/1 stick unsalted butter, diced
1 medium free-range egg, beaten
extra virgin olive oil
60g/2¼ oz/⅓ cup freshly grated
   Parmesan cheese

1–2 tablespoons tapenade (black-olive paste)
800g/1 lb 12 oz (about 8–10) vine-ripened
   tomatoes, thickly sliced and patted dry
250g/9 oz black pudding, sliced,
   or 115g/4 oz (a handful) rocket
sea salt and freshly ground black pepper

1 Grease a shallow 28cm/11 in tart tin. For the pastry, place the flour, oatmeal and a pinch of salt in a food processor with the butter. Process briefly until the mixture resembles breadcrumbs, or rub in the mixture by hand. Add the egg through the feeder tube, or add while stirring. Add about 1 teaspoon oil until the mixture comes together in large clumps. Wrap in clingfilm and chill for 30 minutes or so. Roll out to cover the base and sides of the tart tin. Prick the base all over, then chill well, preferably overnight.

2 Preheat the oven to 200°C/400°F/Gas 6. Fill the pastry case with foil and baking beans, and bake blind for 15 minutes. Remove the foil and beans and continue to cook for a further 5 minutes before removing. While the pastry is still hot scatter over the cheese and leave to cool.

3 Dot over the tapenade. Lay the tomatoes on top in tight concentric circles, so they sit up proud. Season well with sea salt and ground pepper. Bake for 30 minutes then remove.

4 Meanwhile, if using black pudding, preheat the grill to hot. Heat 1 tablespoon oil in a frying pan then, once very hot, add the slices and fry for a couple of minutes on each side or until crispy. Place the black pudding slices on top of the tart in a circle, and grill for 2 minutes until it becomes slightly crisp and golden on top. If using rocket, pile the rocket in the middle of the tart (and, of course, don't grill!). Serve warm with salad.

QUICHE LORRAINE

Quiche Lorraine has come a long way since its origins in the sixteenth century. Then it was simply a sensible way to use up local produce: bacon, cream and eggs were baked on a bread dough base (not in a tart tin), rather like Neapolitan pizza – bread topped with tomatoes and olive oil – or Provence's pissaladière with onions, anchovies and olives. Over the years the bread in the quiche gave way to a lighter pastry – either *pâte brisée* or *pâte feuilletée* and tart tins were introduced.

Since the 1960s and 1970s when UK wine bars began serving up quiche in earnest, diners have witnessed some exceedingly grim offerings. Great wedges of chilled rubbery filling on soggy, uncooked pastry have, for some inexplicable reason, been accepted in this country.

The authentic French Quiche Lorraine, however, is served fresh from the oven, hot and with nothing more than a simple salad of floppy lettuce dressed in oil, vinegar and Dijon mustard. So forget the baked potato, coleslaw and pickle – and concentrate on the classic: a crispy pastry case filled with only three ingredients (four if milk is used, as I prefer, to lighten the cream). The classic is truly a dish worthy of a eulogy: the soggy, chilled Quiche is Dead; Long Live the Quiche.

SERVES 6

200g/7 oz/1³/₄ cups plain flour, sifted

100g/3¹/₂ oz/1 stick unsalted butter, diced

¹/₂ teaspoon salt

200g/7 oz smoked streaky bacon, diced

150ml/5 fl oz/²/₃ cup double cream

300ml/¹/₂ pint/1¹/₃ cups milk

4 large free-range eggs

salt and freshly ground black pepper

1 Make the pastry in the usual way: in a food processor, process the flour, butter and salt then slowly add enough water to combine to a soft but not sticky ball (about 50ml/2 fl oz/ ¹/₄ cup). Alternatively, by hand, rub the butter into the flour with the salt then gradually incorporate the water.

2 Wrap in clingfilm and chill for 30 minutes. Butter a 23cm/9 in shallow metal tart tin. Roll out the pastry to line the tin, prick the base and chill well, preferably overnight to prevent shrinkage.

3 Preheat the oven to 200°C/400°F/Gas 6. Fill the pastry shell with foil and baking beans and bake for 15 minutes. Remove the foil and beans and continue to cook for a further 5 minutes, then remove. Reduce the heat to 190°C/375°F/Gas 5.

4 Fry the bacon (without extra fat) in a hot frying pan until golden brown, then drain away any fat and place the bacon in the pastry base. Beat together the cream, milk and eggs, season generously with salt and pepper and pour slowly over the bacon. Carefully place in the oven and bake for 35–40 minutes until golden brown. Eat warm.

CRAB AND SPINACH TART

I prefer to use mainly white crabmeat for this recipe, but if you are starting from scratch – that is with a live crab – then use everything, brown and white. Serve with a well-dressed salad.

SERVES 6

175g/6 oz/1$\frac{1}{2}$ cups plain flour, sifted
50g/1$\frac{3}{4}$ oz/$\frac{1}{3}$ cup, plus 2 teaspoons, polenta
$\frac{1}{2}$ teaspoon salt
125g/4$\frac{1}{2}$ oz/1$\frac{1}{4}$ sticks unsalted butter, chilled and diced
1 large free-range egg
1 tablespoon olive oil

FOR THE FILLING
1 tablespoon olive oil
2 large garlic cloves, peeled and chopped
225g/8 oz (2 handfuls) young spinach, washed
250g/9 oz ricotta cheese
2 large free-range eggs
$\frac{1}{4}$ teaspoon freshly grated nutmeg
200g/7 oz fresh crabmeat (or use frozen, thoroughly drained and patted dry)
salt and freshly ground black pepper

1 To make the pastry, place the flour, the 50g/1$\frac{3}{4}$ oz/$\frac{1}{3}$ cup polenta, the salt and the butter in a food processor and combine until the mixture resembles breadcrumbs, or rub in the mixture by hand. Mix the egg and oil together in a bowl and add through the feeder tube, or add while stirring. Process only briefly, until the mixture will draw together into a ball in your hands. Wrap in clingfilm and chill for at least 1 hour.

2 Butter a deep, 23cm/9 in flan tin. Roll out the pastry to fit and prick the base with a fork. Leave to chill in the refrigerator for at least 2 hours, or preferably overnight.

3 Preheat the oven to 190°C/375°F/Gas 5. Fill the pastry base with foil and baking beans and bake for 15 minutes, then remove the foil and beans and continue to bake for 5 minutes until the base is lightly cooked. Cool the base slightly.

4 To make the filling, heat the oil in a large pan and sauté the garlic for about 2 minutes, then add the spinach, stirring to coat. After about 2 minutes it will have wilted and cooked down. Remove the pan from the heat. In a bowl, beat together the ricotta cheese, eggs and nutmeg until smooth, using a balloon whisk. Add plenty of salt and pepper. Stir in the contents of the spinach pan and combine well.

5 To assemble, sprinkle the 2 teaspoons polenta over the pastry base. Top with the well-drained crabmeat. Spoon over the spinach filling, spreading it gently over.

6 Bake for about 40 minutes or until tinged with golden brown. Leave for at least 20 minutes then cut into slices and eat warm.

TUNA AND ARTICHOKE TART

This tasty tart is action-packed! Full of chunky pieces of artichoke and tuna, it is wonderful served warm for lunch with salad and bread – or as a starter for dinner, perhaps with a dollop of home-made mayonnaise made with half sunflower oil and half pistachio oil.

SERVES 6

200g/7 oz/1$^3/_4$ cups plain flour, sifted

25g/1 oz/2 tablespoons freshly grated
    Parmesan cheese

$^1/_2$ teaspoon salt

125g/4$^1/_2$ oz/1$^1/_4$ sticks unsalted butter,
    chilled and diced

1 medium free-range egg

1–2 tablespoons olive oil

FOR THE FILLING

200ml/7 fl oz crème fraîche

3 medium free-range eggs

grated zest of 1 large unwaxed lemon

2 tablespoons flat leaf parsley leaves,
    finely chopped

290g/10$^1/_4$ oz artichoke hearts in oil, drained
    and chopped

400g/14 oz tinned tuna, drained and flaked
    into chunks

salt and freshly ground black pepper

1 Lightly butter a deep 23cm/9 in flan tin. To make the pastry, place the flour, Parmesan, salt and the butter in a food processor and process briefly until the mixture resembles breadcrumbs, or rub in the mixture by hand. In a bowl, mix together the egg with 1 tablespoon oil and, with the machine running, slowly add this through the feeder tube. Process until the mixture looks moist, adding a little more oil if necessary, or add the egg and oil while stirring. Gather the dough together with your hands and wrap in clingfilm. Chill for 1 hour.

2 Roll out to fit the flan tin and prick the base all over with a fork. Place in the refrigerator for at least 2 hours, or preferably overnight, to prevent shrinkage.

3 Preheat the oven to 200°C/400°F/Gas 6. Line the pastry shell with foil and baking beans and bake blind for 15 minutes. Remove the foil and beans and return to the oven for a further 5 minutes.

4 Remove and cool for at least 15 minutes. Reduce the oven temperature to 190°C/375°F/Gas 5. To make the filling, beat together the crème fraîche, eggs, lemon zest, parsley and plenty of salt and pepper.

5 Place the chopped artichokes on the pastry base, then top with the tuna. Pour over the crème fraîche mixture and bake for about 40 minutes until puffed up and golden brown. Cool in the tin for at least 30 minutes before transferring to a serving plate.

PARMESAN TARTLETS WITH MORELS AND ASPARAGUS

These are tasty little tartlets, ideal as a starter for a light main course – or for lunch on their own – in springtime, of course, when local asparagus is in season.

Morels are the first wild mushrooms to be in season; from March through to May in the UK. If using fresh (use about 125g/4½ oz and omit the soaking), you must clean them thoroughly as tiny bugs or loose bits of soil can lurk in the cavities.

SERVES 4

100g/3½ oz/1 scant cup plain flour, sifted
100g/3½ oz/⅔ cup freshly grated
   Parmesan cheese
100g/3½ oz/1 stick unsalted butter, diced
1 medium free-range egg

FOR THE FILLING
40g/1½ oz dried morels (or porcini/ceps)
150ml/5 fl oz/⅔ cup white wine
150g/5½ oz asparagus, halved
25g/1 oz/¼ stick unsalted butter
1 garlic clove, peeled and crushed
150ml/5 fl oz/⅔ cup double cream
salt and freshly ground black pepper

1 Place the flour, Parmesan and a pinch of salt in a food processor with the butter. Process briefly until blended, then add the egg and 1 tablespoon cold water. Alternatively, rub the butter into the dry ingredients by hand and stir in the egg and 1 tbsp water.

2 Process briefly then gather the dough in your hands and wrap in clingfilm. Chill for 1 hour. Butter four 10cm/4 in springform tart tins, then roll out the pastry to fit. (You can cut the excess pastry into rounds and bake as Parmesan shortbread – see page 127.) Prick the base, and chill for at least 2 hours or overnight.

3 Preheat the oven to 200°C/400°F/Gas 6. Fill each tart with foil and baking beans and bake for 15 minutes, then remove the foil and beans and cook for a further 5–10 minutes until cooked. Cool.

4 To make the filling, rinse the dried mushrooms and soak in the wine for 30 minutes. Drain, reserving the soaking liquor. Cook the asparagus for 3–4 minutes until just tender then plunge into cold water. Pat dry.

5 Melt the butter, and gently fry the garlic for 1 minute, then add the mushrooms and gently fry for 10 minutes, stirring. Add the soaking liquor (or wine if you are using fresh mushrooms). Cook over a high heat for 3 minutes until evaporated. Stir in the cream and asparagus and cook gently for 3–4 minutes until hot. Season to taste.

6 Fill each tart with the asparagus mixture and serve at once.

MEAT PIES

The idea for this pie comes from two places: Scotland and Australia. Firstly, Scotland: on New Year's Day we traditionally serve up steak pie (indeed it used also to be served on Christmas Day in many families). It is a thick chunky beef stew covered in puff pastry and served with mashed potatoes and marrowfat (or mushy) peas, known as buster peas in my home town of Dundee.

The Australian connection is that in Adelaide there are two pie carts that set up in the city each evening: Balfours at the railway station and Vilis at Victoria Square. These are the only two pie carts left, though in their heyday (they have been in Adelaide since 1915) there were about 30. On my last trip to that gourmet city, I opted for the Mini Floater – a smaller version of the mighty Pie Floater but essentially the same. It is a meat pie filled with chunky beef, with a shortcrust base and puff pastry top. The pie is inverted, piping hot, into a disposable dish with a flood of thick pea soup ladled on top; it is finished off with a squoosh of tomato ketchup. (To make the pea soup, soak 400g/14 oz dried green split peas overnight then rinse. Melt 25g/1 oz butter and gently cook 200g/7 oz smoked bacon and 1 peeled, chopped onion until soft then add the peas, 1 litre/1³/₄ pints hot ham stock and 2 tablespoons mustard. Bring to the boil, then simmer for 45 minutes or until cooked. Liquidise then season to taste.) The floater is usually taken late at night and it is certainly not unusual to see party goers, sometimes in black tie and long dresses, stand at tables set up beside the carts with their plastic spoons, tucking into this most delicious of late-night fare.

I have devised a recipe of four individual pies that can be served as we would in Scotland on 1 January, with mash and mushy peas, or with thick pea soup for a true South Australian pie floater.

I make the pies in little round pie tins (about 200ml/7 fl oz capacity), measuring about 13cm/5 in across the top. But if you can find rectangular foil containers, that would make them more authentic for serving as pie floaters with pea soup, as the Adelaide pies are rectangular or oval, never round.

MAKES 4

25g/1 oz/¹/₄ stick unsalted butter

450g/1 lb stewing beef (chuck or shoulder), diced

2 tablespoons plain flour, seasoned with salt and pepper

1 teaspoon olive oil

1 medium onion, peeled and finely chopped

2 small carrots, peeled and diced

300ml/¹/₂ pint/1¹/₃ cups hot beef stock

1 heaped tablespoon tomato purée

¹/₂ tablespoon Worcestershire sauce

FOR THE PASTRY

50g/1³/₄ oz/¹/₂ cup unbleached strong white flour

70g/2¹/₂ oz/²/₃ cup plain flour

60g/2¹/₄ oz/¹/₂ stick unsalted butter, diced

175g/6 oz ready-rolled puff pastry, thawed if frozen

1 medium free-range egg, beaten

1 First make the stew: melt the butter in a wide pan. Toss the beef in the seasoned flour, then brown all over. Remove with a slotted spoon. Add the oil and gently fry the onion and carrots for a few minutes. Return the meat to the pan and add the hot stock, tomato purée and Worcestershire sauce. Stir and reduce the heat to the lowest setting. Cover and cook on the hob for 1 hour. Remove from the heat, taste and adjust the seasoning. Leave to cool. Cover and chill overnight.

2 Butter four baking tins. To make the shortcrust pastry: sift the strong and plain flours into a food processor with a pinch of salt, and add the butter. Process briefly until the mixture resembles breadcrumbs, then add about 2 tablespoons cold water – just enough so that you can bring the mixture together with your hands. Alternatively, rub the butter into the dry ingredients by hand.

3 Wrap in clingfilm and chill for 30 minutes. Roll out the pastry to fit the bases and sides of the tins. Fill each with the stew.

4 Cut out the ready-rolled puff pastry to fit the tops of each tin and place on top, pressing the edges well together. Pinch the edges to seal, then chill the pies again, preferably for a couple of hours. Remove to room temperature at least 30 minutes before baking. Meanwhile, preheat the oven to 200°C/400°F/Gas 6 and heat a baking sheet.

5 Brush the pies with egg and then snip a small hole in the top with scissors. Place the pies directly on to the heated baking sheet so that the shortcrust pastry will begin to cook immediately. Bake for 25–30 minutes until puffed up and golden brown.

6 Leave the pies for a couple of minutes before turning them out carefully from the tins. Serve with mashed potatoes and stir-fried cabbage. Alternatively, if you are serving as floaters, fill a large soup dish with thick pea soup, invert the pie into it, so that the puff side is down and the shortcrust on top. Top with a squoosh of ketchup and devour with a spoon.

CORNISH PASTY

This makes one rather large pasty, which easily feeds two people. You can make two smaller ones, if you prefer, but it is difficult to achieve such a moist filling if they are smaller.

My recipe is based on a recipe from The Lizard Pasty Shop, the most southerly Cornish pasty shop in the country. Just to confuse everyone, the Cornish and the Scots call swedes turnips (with the Scots also calling them neeps), but I have bowed to the majority and used the word swedes in the recipe below. The traditional pasty is made only with skirt beef, onion, turnip (swede) and potato, which should all be very well seasoned. The pastry, made from strong white (bread) flour is light, crisp and flaky. The crimping technique, used to seal the pasty, makes the final product look authentic. It is not difficult: simply fold the pastry edge over in a rope pattern, tucking in the end when you reach the other side. It is important not to prick a hole in the top before baking, for the method of cooking the filling is almost 'pressure-cooking': the juices are sealed inside, to provide the most succulent filling.

MAKES 1 LARGE PASTY

225g/8 oz/2 scant cups unbleached strong
   white flour, sifted
½ teaspoon salt
115g/4 oz/1 stick unsalted butter, cubed

FOR THE FILLING (peeled and prepared weights)
25g/1 oz onion, peeled and finely chopped

50g/1¾ oz swede, peeled and finely chopped
85–115g/3–4 oz skirt beef, cut into
   small pieces
1 tablespoon whole flat leaf parsley leaves
125–150g/4½–5½ oz potato, finely chopped
beaten egg or milk, to glaze
salt and freshly ground black pepper

1 Make the pastry by placing the flour and salt in a food processor and process briefly. Then add the butter and process until the mixture resembles breadcrumbs. Add sufficient water (1½–2 tablespoons) to combine to a ball. Alternatively, rub the butter into the dry ingredients by hand and stir in the water. Cover and chill for about 30 minutes. Meanwhile, preheat the oven to 220°C/425°F/Gas 7.

2 Roll out the pastry to a 23cm/9 in round. Trim around the edges with a plate to form a neat circle. Place the onion and swede on one half of the circle, then season well. Place the meat on top, season again, then top with whole parsley leaves. Top with the potatoes and season again. Press the filling down well as you go.

3 Moisten one half of the circle edge with water, then fold over the other half to seal. Crimp the edges, as described above (do not make a steam hole). Transfer to a lightly greased baking tray and brush with egg or milk, to glaze. Bake for 10 minutes, then turn the oven down to 180°C/350°F/Gas 4 for a further 45 minutes. Serve warm or cold.

FORFAR BRIDIES

Bridies and pies are still very much a part of life in Dundee and Angus, just like pasties are in Cornwall. And whereas the best pies have traditionally come from Dundee, the best bridies are from Forfar. J. M. Barrie mentioned bridies in one of the novels he wrote at the turn of the last century. He was native of Kirriemuir, some five miles north-west of Forfar and so would have been very familiar with the bridies of Angus.

My recipe is based on Bill McLaren's, whose great-grandfather, James, learned the skills of bridie-making at Jolly's bakery. His family-run bakery – opened in 1893 – has baked bridies to the same recipe ever since. On a visit there, he taught me about the essential 'dunting' and 'nicking' procedure to seal the horseshoe-shaped bridie. The 'dunting' is done with the heel of the hand, pressing down on the edges. The 'nicking' is done with forefinger and thumb, to finish the sealing. Unlike the pasty, the bridie is pricked with a characteristic hole prior to baking.

MAKES 4

FOR THE PASTRY	FOR THE FILLING
250g/9 oz/2 cups unbleached strong white flour	450g/1 lb shoulder or rump beef
75g/2¾ oz/⅔ cup plain flour	85g/3 oz beef suet, grated
175g/6 oz/1¼ stick unsalted butter, cubed	1 small onion, peeled and finely grated
	salt and freshly ground black pepper

1 To make the pastry, sift the flours and a pinch of salt into a food processor. Add the butter and process until incorporated. Add just enough cold water (2½–3 tablespoons) to bind to a stiff dough. Alternatively, rub the butter into the dry ingredients by hand and stir in the water. Gather the dough in your hands, wrap in clingfilm and chill for at least 1 hour.

2 To make the filling, roughly chop the beef – I use the pulse button on my food processor. Alternatively, mince very coarsely. Mix together the beef, suet, onion and plenty of salt and pepper. The mixture should be fairly stiff.

3 Divide the pastry into four and roll each piece into an oval. Divide the filling into four and spoon on to one half of each pastry oval, leaving a border all round.

4 Dampen the edges and fold the top half of the pastry over the filling to enclose it. Trim the edges into a neat horseshoe shape (not a half-moon: that is the Cornish pasty). Now 'dunt' and 'nick', by pressing down the edges to seal and crimping all around to give a nicely finished look. Using a sharp knife, make a small hole for the steam to escape in the top of each bridie. Place on a lightly buttered baking tray and chill for an hour or so. Meanwhile, preheat the oven to 200°C/400°F/Gas 6.

5 Bake for about 40 minutes, or until a pale golden brown. Serve warm.

CULLEN SKINK BRIDIES

This delicious variation on the classic Forfar bridie uses the primary ingredients in one of Scotland's most famous soups, Cullen Skink, a hearty meal-in-a-bowl made with finnan haddock, potatoes, onions and milk.

MAKES 4

1 × pastry from page 47
500g/1lb 2 oz undyed smoked haddock fillets
300ml/½ pint/1⅓ cups milk
20g/¾ oz flat leaf parsley, leaves chopped,
   stalks retained

25g/1 oz/¼ stick unsalted butter
25g/1 oz/2 tablespoons plain flour
2 heaped teaspoons Dijon mustard
grated zest of 1 unwaxed lemon
salt and freshly ground black pepper

1 Make the pastry as on page 47.

2 Place the fish in a pan with the milk and parsley stalks. Bring slowly to the boil, bubble for 1 minute, then remove from the heat and cover. Leave for 30 minutes or so, then strain through a sieve over a jug. Melt the butter in a pan, add the flour, stir for 1 minute, then add the reserved fish liquor. Cook, whisking constantly, over a medium to low heat until smooth. Stir in the mustard, lemon zest, chopped parsley leaves, flaked fish and seasoning to taste. Cool.

3 Make the bridies as on page 47, using this fish filling instead of the meat filling.

CHEESE EMPANADAS

These cheese empanadas are based on some wonderful Chilean pies I ate while visiting the country's main market, housed in its own Victorian building constructed in 1890, in downtown Santiago. Having got up at the crack of dawn to miss the rush hour on the city's underground, I was beginning to feel famished as I trawled round the stalls admiring the wonderful asparagus, raspberries, blueberries, beans and fresh herbs. The fish stalls were full of prehistoric-looking creatures that I thought existed only in Steven Spielberg movies. The meat stalls were equally fascinating but none of these was doing my state of raging hunger any good. It is a well-known fact that when in doubt about where to find good food abroad, follow the locals. My search did not take long, for just outside the market was a long queue at a little empanada stall. There was plenty of time for deliberation, but only two choices: *empanada de queso* (cheese) or *empanada de pino* (meat, onion and spices). In the interest of research, I decided to have both. The meat pie, made from a shortcrust pastry, was filled with a delicious onion-laden stew, one-fifth of a hard-boiled egg and two raisins, with one shiny black olive neatly tucked into one corner. The cheese pie, in puff pastry, was filled with grated cheese, pure and simple. And it was divine. I have tried to reproduce it in the recipe below and I must say, it tastes rather good. Emmenthal is the closest equivalent to the flavour of the Chilean cheese; otherwise mozzarella will do for the gooey texture.

MAKES 4

375g/13 oz ready-rolled puff pastry, thawed if frozen

150g/5$\frac{1}{2}$ oz Swiss Emmenthal cheese, grated
1 small free-range egg, beaten

1 Lay the puff pastry out on a surface. Cover one half lengthways with the cheese, leaving a narrow border around the edges. Dampen the edges with a little water and fold over the other half. Press down all around to seal. Using a sharp knife, cut into four. Seal all the other edges and transfer the empanadas to an oiled baking sheet. Brush the tops with beaten egg. Chill for at least 1 hour. Meanwhile, preheat the oven to 220°C/425°F/Gas 7.

2 Brush the empanadas again with egg (glazing them twice gives them a lovely glossy coat). Bake for about 20 minutes until puffed up and golden brown. Eat at once.

MINI GOAT'S CHEESE STRUDELS

These are tasty little pastries that are perfect as canapés served with a nice glass of something cold – if not champagne, I'd recommend Sancerre, which works well with goat's cheese. Or you can cut them into larger pieces and serve as a starter with a salad of floppy-leafed lettuce dressed in walnut oil.

MAKES 12

4 large sheets of filo pastry (about 125g/ 4$\frac{1}{2}$ oz), thawed if frozen

40g/1$\frac{1}{2}$ oz/$\frac{1}{2}$ stick unsalted butter, melted

2 tablespoons freshly grated Parmesan cheese

150g/5$\frac{1}{2}$ oz soft, mild goat's cheese

2 teaspoons fresh thyme leaves, chopped

salt and freshly ground black pepper

1 Preheat the oven to 220°C/425°F/Gas 7 and lightly grease a baking sheet.

2 Lay the first sheet of filo out on a board then, working quickly (and keeping the other sheets covered), brush all over with the melted butter. Top with another sheet, and brush with more butter. Top with a third sheet, brush with butter, then sprinkle over the Parmesan. Top with the fourth sheet, then spread the goat's cheese carefully over. (This can be spread on the top half only as it will all be rolled up anyway.) Season, and sprinkle over the thyme.

3 Roll up from the long end to make a long roly-poly. Cut into 12 pieces, either straight or slanted, and lay them on the baking sheet. Brush lightly with butter. Bake for 12–15 minutes until golden brown. Eat warm. (See page 52 for image.)

ANCHOVY PIROZHKIS

These dinky little patties are based on Russian *pirozhkis* – tiny pies served with broth or soup. I remember in the late 1970s during a visit to pre-Glasnost Moscow being served cabbage *pirozhkis* with tea fresh from the samovar in my hotel. And although the words 'cabbage pie' conjure up visions of a rather depressing Solzhenitsynesque scene rather than an inspiring gastronomic vignette, they were truly delicious.

The following recipe is based on my Finnish friend Ritva's recipe, which she used to serve with borscht. I suggest either serving them with a thick warming soup or as substantial canapés with drinks, preferably champanski!

MAKES 20–22

250g/9 oz/2 cups plain flour, sifted
½ teaspoon salt
175g/6 oz/1¾ sticks unsalted butter, chilled, diced
1 large free-range egg yolk

FOR THE FILLING
50g/1¾ oz canned anchovies in olive oil
2 large hard-boiled eggs, mashed
1 tablespoon Dijon mustard
2 heaped tablespoons mayonnaise
freshly ground black pepper

1 To make the pastry, place the flour and salt in a food processor then add the butter. Process briefly until the mixture resembles breadcrumbs, then add the egg yolk and 40–50ml/ 1½–2 fl oz/about ¼ cup cold water. You need enough water so that when you stop the machine you can bring the dough into a ball with your hands. Alternatively, rub the butter into the dry ingredients by hand and stir in the egg yolk and water. Wrap the dough in clingfilm and chill for an hour or so.

2 To make the filling, drain the anchovies but retain the oil. Finely chop them and mix with the eggs, mustard and mayonnaise. Season with pepper.

3 Roll out the pastry thinly, then cut out 20–22 pastry circles using a large pastry cutter or upturned glass (about 9–10cm/3½–4 in diameter).

4 Place 1 heaped teaspoon of filling on one side of each circle. Fold over to form a half-moon and seal the edges using the tines of a fork. Using a pastry brush, brush the tops with some of the reserved anchovy oil. Place on a lightly buttered baking sheet and chill for about 30 minutes. Meanwhile, preheat the oven to 220°C/425°F/Gas 7.

5 Bake for 15 minutes or until a light golden brown. Remove to a wire rack to cool then serve barely warm.

PIZZETTE

These are handy little canapés for kids and grown-ups alike, but probably made with kids in mind. At my daughter Faith's 18th birthday barbecue we had these as canapés before the barbecue began. I say 'we' but in fact I was exiled to the upper floor of our house while the 'young' stayed downstairs . . . the deal was, if I was needed to come down to check out the food – and guests – I had to phone down first. Those who know me well will know whether I was likely to do so or not.

MAKES 45–50

500g/1 lb 2 oz/4$^1/_3$ cups unbleached strong white flour	**FOR THE TOPPINGS**
2 teaspoons salt	passata (about 175g/6 oz/1$^1/_2$ cups)
2 × 7g/$^1/_4$ oz sachets of fast-action/easy-blend dried yeast	pesto sauce (about 100g/3$^1/_2$ oz/1 scant cup)
	150–200g/5$^1/_2$–7 oz mozzarella cheese, grated
2 tablespoons olive oil	olive oil
	salt and freshly ground black pepper

1 Place the flour in a bowl with the salt. Stir in the yeast then make a well in the centre. Add the olive oil and about 350ml/12 fl oz/1$^1/_2$ cups tepid water – enough to make a fairly soft dough. Turn on to a floured surface and knead gently until smooth, about 8–10 minutes.

2 Place in a bowl, cover with oiled clingfilm and leave in a warm place for an hour until risen.

3 Knock back the dough and place on a floured surface. Roll out until fairly thin. Grease several baking sheets. Cut into 45–50 discs using a small round pastry cutter and place these on the baking sheets. Cover loosely with oiled clingfilm and leave for 30 minutes or so. Meanwhile, preheat the oven to 230°C/450°F/Gas 8.

4 To make the toppings: spoon about a teaspoon of passata on to each pizzette, then add $^1/_2$ teaspoon of pesto and some cheese. Season with salt and pepper, then bake for about 10 minutes or until well risen.

5 Remove from the oven, then, using a teaspoon, drip one drop of olive oil over each pizzette. Transfer to a serving plate. Serve warm.

Optional toppings

- black olives, pitted and sliced
- sun-dried tomatoes, sliced
- salami, cut into pieces
- mushrooms, chopped and lightly sautéed
- artichoke hearts, cooked and chopped

GOUGÈRES WITH KIR

I first came across gougères in the Burgundian city of Dijon, famous for its mustard and also for these fabulous puffs of cheese, served warm in restaurants with Kir. Canon Felix Kir, formerly a village priest, became mayor of Dijon just after the Second World War in recognition of his activities as a resistance fighter. For over 20 years – until his death in 1968 – he entertained visiting dignitaries to cocktail parties at the town hall. Champagne and martinis had been the order of the day until he decided, in 1952, that, since they were in the heart of Burgundy, they should serve only local wines. He therefore insisted that the local white wine – Aligoté – be mixed with crème de cassis, a blackcurrant liqueur made in Dijon. Since Aligoté makes a fairly tart wine, it provides the perfect balance for the sweetness of crème de cassis. This cocktail was not the Canon's own invention: 'vin blanc cassis' had been drunk for many years in Paris, but he popularised it locally. Such was his fame and reputation during the war years that his name gradually became closely linked with the drink all over France. People began to ask for 'Canon Kir's drink', then 'a Canon Kir', then simply 'a Kir'.

MAKES 12

55g/2 oz/$^1/_2$ stick unsalted butter
85g/3 oz/$^3/_4$ cup plain flour, sifted
2 medium free-range eggs

85g/3 oz/$^3/_4$ cup grated Comté cheese (or half French Emmenthal and half mature Cheddar)
freshly grated nutmeg

1 Preheat the oven to 200°C/400°F/Gas 6 and lightly butter and flour a baking tray.

2 Place the butter and 150ml/5 fl oz/$^2/_3$ cup cold water in a heavy-based pan and heat slowly until the butter melts. Now bring to a rapid boil and remove immediately from the heat. Quickly tip in all the flour and return to a low heat. Beat vigorously until the mixture comes away clean from the sides of the pan; this will take 1 to 2 minutes. Remove from the heat and cool for about 1 minute.

3 Add one egg, beating hard to ensure it is completely amalgamated, before adding the second. Beat well until smooth and glossy. Stir in the cheese, a tiny grating of nutmeg and a pinch of salt.

4 Using two teaspoons, heap 12 blobs of the mixture on to the baking tray, spacing well apart. Bake for about 30 minutes or until puffed up and golden brown all over.

5 Just before the gougères are ready to come out of the oven, pour about 50ml/2 fl oz/$^1/_4$ cup of cassis into each wine glass. Top up with about 150ml/5 fl oz/$^2/_3$ cup of the wine (or champagne for Kir Royal).

6 Transfer the gougères to a wire rack and, using a sharp knife, pierce a tiny hole in the side of each one, to release any steam. Serve barely warm with Kir.

Sweet pies, pastries and tarts

Everyone enjoys sweet pies and tarts. But some completely sane people come over all emotional when confronted with a certain pie. I can still taste the exquisitely sweet cinnamon apples and crunchy topping on my mum's Dutch apple tart. I have a friend who is so enamoured of blackcurrant pie he will phone his friends just before he is about to sit down and eat it – to share his joy vicariously. Another friend, usually reserved and composed, becomes almost weepy at the prospect of gooseberry tart, just like his mother used to make. Many would never consider having any other restaurant dessert than lemon tart.

The way pie is eaten is also interesting: some like it hot with custard, some warm with cream, thick or pouring. My father-in-law, John, only likes pies cold, but a scoop of ice cream is his favourite accompaniment. This is also mine, although I like my pie hot, as the sensation of warm sweet filling and lightly crusted buttery pastry combined with a cold creamy ice melting all over is too near my idea of perfection for words. Which is why I say nothing and just eat ∎

PECAN TASSIES

These are tiny little pecan pies – the word 'tassie' a diminutive of tartlet from the southern states of America. Although I absolutely adore pecan pie it can be incredibly rich, and so here is the perfect solution – a sensible two-bitesize offering. Except that they are so good you will then want another.

You will need two 12 hole, deep bun tins for these.

MAKES 18

150g/5$\frac{1}{2}$ oz/1$\frac{1}{4}$ cups plain flour, sifted
25g/1 oz/2 tablespoons golden caster sugar
50g/1$\frac{3}{4}$ oz/$\frac{1}{2}$ cup ground almonds
85g/3 oz/$\frac{3}{4}$ stick unsalted butter, diced
1 medium free-range egg, beaten
2 teaspoons lemon juice

FOR THE FILLING

70g/2$\frac{1}{2}$ oz/$\frac{3}{4}$ stick unsalted butter, melted
50g/1$\frac{3}{4}$ oz/$\frac{1}{4}$ cup light muscovado sugar
2 medium free-range eggs, beaten
2 tablespoons golden syrup
juice of $\frac{1}{2}$ lemon
100g/3$\frac{1}{2}$ oz/$\frac{3}{4}$ cup shelled pecan nuts, chopped

1 Place the flour, sugar, almonds and butter in a food processor and process briefly, or rub in the mixture by hand. Add the egg and lemon juice through the feeder tube, then bring together with your hands, or add while stirring. Wrap in clingfilm and chill briefly.

2 Thinly roll out the pastry and cut into 18 circles using a 7–8cm/2$\frac{3}{4}$–3$\frac{1}{4}$ in pastry cutter. Place in the tins, pressing gently to fit. Prick the base of each with a fork and chill for at least 2 hours, preferably overnight.

3 Preheat the oven to 190°C/375°F/Gas 5. Beat the butter, sugar, eggs, golden syrup and lemon juice together, and add the pecan nuts. Fill each pastry case with this mixture.

4 Bake for 15–20 minutes until golden brown. Cool in the tin for 10 minutes, then turn out and leave to cool.

BAKEWELL TART

The popular Bakewell tart is now so called because it is made in a pastry case, but the original Derbyshire dish was in fact Bakewell pudding, and one with a most interesting – if apocryphal – story to it. In the middle of the nineteenth century, a cook at The Rutland Arms, Bakewell, mistook her mistress's instructions to make a rich jam tart, and from this apparently grave error, a pudding of jam and almondy cream topping was created.

Now, of course, there are many variations. The most common one – puff pastry spread with jam and topped with almond-flavoured cake mix – is tasty for tea-time; although admittedly it is more jam tart than the original Derbyshire almond-flavoured pudding.

My version uses a crisp shortcrust instead of puff pastry and is made in a round, instead of the traditional oval.

SERVES 6–8

150g/5½ oz/1¼ cups plain flour, sifted
55g/2 oz/½ cup ground almonds
85g/3 oz/¾ stick unsalted butter, diced
1 large free-range egg

FOR THE FILLING
2–3 tablespoons strawberry jam
85g/3 oz/¾ stick unsalted butter
85g/3 oz/⅓ cup golden caster sugar
3 medium free-range eggs

1 Butter a 20cm/8 in fluted flan tin. Place the flour, a pinch of salt and the almonds in a food processor and add the butter. Process until it resembles breadcrumbs, or rub in the mixture by hand.

2 Beat the egg lightly and add through the feeder tube while the machine is running, or add while stirring. Bring the dough together with your hands and wrap in clingfilm. Chill for about 1 hour.

3 Roll out the dough to line the base and sides of the prepared tin. Prick the base and chill for at least 2 hours, or preferably overnight.

4 Preheat the oven to 190°C/375°F/Gas 5. Fill the pastry case with foil and baking beans, and bake blind for 15 minutes. Remove the foil and beans and bake for a further 5 minutes. Allow to cool slightly.

5 Increase the oven temperature to 200°C/400°F/Gas 6. Spread the base with the strawberry jam. Melt the butter and sugar together in a small pan, remove from the heat and then beat in the eggs. Whisk together until thoroughly combined.

6 Pour this mixture over the jam, and bake for about 20 minutes until the top is a light golden brown. Serve warm or at room temperature.

APPLE PIE

Appel taart is a family favourite in Holland, often made when visitors come for morning coffee. It is also served for celebrations, always with plenty of whipped cream. I recently had a delicious one topped with a layer of glazed nuts at Amsterdam's Schiphol airport.

My recipe is based on one from my Dutch friend, Mary-An. Her father, Cornelius, fondly remembers these huge pies from his childhood. Since he was one of 13 children, everything came in vast quantities, including huge apple tarts, which were treats for birthdays only.

This may seem like a lot of apples to pack into one tin but since they are cooking apples, they all squish down into a fluffy mass, the perfect contrast to the short, sweet pastry. And do not be put off by the prospect of making a lattice top. The correct way is to place half the strips from left to right over the tart. Then fold back every other strip halfway. Place a strip across the unfolded strips from front to back, before unfolding the strips. Then fold back the alternate strips, and continue until the lattice is finished. Or, an easier way is simply to place one strip across the top edge of the tart. Then place another at right angles and place it over the first strip, then continue until they are all finished, remembering to start at alternate sides of the tart each time. The result – although not authentically 'woven' – looks perfectly acceptable.

SERVES 8–10

280g/10 oz/2$\frac{1}{2}$ scant cups self-raising flour, sifted

175g/6 oz/1$\frac{3}{4}$ sticks unsalted butter, chilled and diced

100g/3$\frac{1}{2}$ oz/scant $\frac{1}{2}$ cup golden caster sugar

FOR THE FILLING

2 teaspoons semolina

1.2 kg/2 lb 10 oz (about 8) large cooking apples

85g/3 oz/$\frac{1}{3}$ cup golden caster sugar

2 heaped teaspoons ground cinnamon

50g/1$\frac{3}{4}$ oz/$\frac{1}{3}$ cup raisins (optional)

1 medium free-range egg white and a little golden caster sugar, to glaze

1 Butter a 24cm/9$\frac{1}{2}$ in springform, deep baking tin.

2 Combine the flour, butter, a pinch of salt and sugar in a food processor. Process until it resembles breadcrumbs, or rub in the mixture by hand. Add sufficient water (75–85ml/ 2$\frac{1}{2}$–3 fl oz/$\frac{1}{3}$–$\frac{1}{2}$ cup) for it to combine to a firm dough. Combine with your hands into a ball, wrap in clingfilm and chill for about 1 hour.

3 Preheat the oven to 200°C/400°F/Gas 6. Roll out two-thirds of the dough on a floured surface, and use it to line the base and sides of the prepared tin. Sprinkle the semolina over the base.

4 Peel and core the apples. Slice them thinly, either using the slicing blade of your food processor or slicing by hand using a sharp knife or a cheese slicer.

5 Combine the sugar and cinnamon together in a small bowl.

6 Put about one-third of the apples into the tin, pressing down gently. Add the raisins, if using. Top with one-third of the sugar mixture. Continue with the remaining apples and sugar, pressing down very gently, to fit them all in.

7 Roll out the remaining pastry to a large, thin rectangle. Set aside a quarter of the pastry. From the remaining pastry, cut out eight strips long enough to make a simple lattice over the top of the apples: place one strip over the apples, then add another at right angles, and so on. With the remaining pastry, make another long strip, and place it over the ends of the strips, to seal around the edges of the pie neatly.

8 Brush with egg white, sprinkle with sugar and bake for 10 minutes. Reduce the temperature to 180°C/350°F/Gas 4, and cook for a further 40–45 minutes, or until the pastry is golden brown and the apples are tender when pierced with the tip of a sharp knife. Cover with foil towards the end of cooking if the top becomes too dark.

9 Remove from the oven and cool for 20–30 minutes, before carefully removing from the tin. Serve warm with thick cream or Greek yogurt.

SOUR CREAM RAISIN PIE

This pie is a luscious, creamy rich affair, one of the most popular of all American pies, standing proudly on the dessert trolley beside pecan, pumpkin, blueberry and apple pies.

For a rum'n'raisin pie, add a good slug of rum to the sour cream mixture and reduce the amount of lemon juice. For a change, make it with a chocolate biscuit crust made by mixing 175–200g/6–7 oz crushed chocolate digestives with 40–50g/$1^{1}/_{2}$–$1^{3}/_{4}$ oz/$^{1}/_{2}$ stick melted butter, then pressing the mixture into the pie tin; chill before filling with the cream mixture.

SERVES 8

150g/$5^{1}/_{2}$ oz/$1^{1}/_{4}$ cups plain flour, sifted

55g/2 oz/$^{1}/_{2}$ cup ground almonds

85g/3 oz/$^{3}/_{4}$ stick unsalted butter, diced

1 large free-range egg

FOR THE FILLING

125g/$4^{1}/_{2}$ oz/generous $^{1}/_{2}$ cup golden caster sugar

2 tablespoons cornflour

2 large free-range eggs, beaten

450ml/16 fl oz soured cream

$1^{1}/_{2}$ tablespoons lemon juice

150g/$5^{1}/_{2}$ oz/1 cup raisins

1 Butter a 23cm/9 in flan tin. Place the flour, a pinch of salt and almonds in a food processor and add the butter. Process until it resembles breadcrumbs, or rub in the mixture by hand.

2 Beat the egg lightly and add through the feeder tube while the machine is running, or add while stirring. Bring the dough together with your hands and wrap in clingfilm. Chill for about 1 hour.

3 Roll out to line the base and sides of the prepared tin. Prick the base and chill for at least 2 hours, or preferably overnight.

4 Preheat the oven to 190°C/375°F/Gas 5. Fill the pastry case with foil and baking beans, and bake blind for 15 minutes. Remove the foil and beans and bake for a further 10 minutes or so, until baked through. Allow to cool slightly.

5 To make the filling, mix the sugar, cornflour and a pinch of salt in a pan. Add the eggs, soured cream and lemon juice, and mix well. Cook over a very low heat for about 10 minutes, stirring continuously, until thickened and smooth.

6 Stir in the raisins, then leave to cool for at least 10 minutes. Pour into the pastry case, cool, and chill for an hour or two before serving.

TREACLE TART

I have never really liked traditional treacle tart because it can so often be cloyingly over-sweet, made as it usually is with simply breadcrumbs, lemon and golden syrup. So this tart is creamier, more lemony and also more treacly because of the inclusion of black treacle as well as golden syrup.

Serve at room temperature or just barely warm, with pouring cream.

SERVES 8

175g/6 oz/1½ cups plain flour, sifted
25g/1 oz/2 tablespoons golden
    caster sugar
100g/3½ oz/1 stick unsalted butter,
    diced
1 large free-range egg yolk

FOR THE FILLING

6 heaped tablespoons golden syrup
1 heaped tablespoon black treacle
juice and grated zest of 2 unwaxed lemons
2 medium free-range eggs, beaten
300ml/½ pint/1⅓ cups double cream

1 Place the flour, sugar, butter and a pinch of salt in a food processor and process briefly. Add the egg yolk through the feeder tube. Alternatively, rub the butter into the dry ingredients by hand and stir in the egg yolk. Gather the mixture together with your hands to form a dough, then wrap in clingfilm and chill for about 1 hour.

2 Lightly butter a shallow 28cm/11 in tart tin, preferably with removable base. Roll out the pastry to fit the prepared tin, prick the base, then chill well – preferably overnight.

3 Preheat the oven to 200°C/400°F/Gas 6. Fill the pastry case with foil and baking beans and bake blind for 15 minutes. Remove the foil and beans and cook for a further 5 minutes. Leave to cool slightly.

4 Reduce the temperature to 170°C/325°F/Gas 3. Gently warm the syrup and treacle (I do this in a microwave on Medium or in a pan over the lowest heat). Stir well, and then stir in the lemon zest and juice. Place a plastic sieve over the bowl or pan and add the beaten eggs. Stir well. (Straining the eggs ensures there are no blobs of egg white that have not been fully incorporated.) Stir in the cream.

5 Once everything is fully combined, tip into the pastry case and bake for 40 minutes or until there is a slight wobble in the centre.

6 Leave to cool before serving.

CHOCOLATE-CRUSTED LEMON TART

This recipe proved extremely popular when I first published it in my *Sunday Times* column over six years ago. It combines two perfect Easter ingredients: chocolate for those people who – like me – have been known to trip up their own children in order to get to the chocolate first during the Easter Bunny Chocolate Egg Hunt in the garden; and lemon – the ideal complement to chocolate. And, of course, lemon is also delicious after roast lamb, making this the perfect dessert to follow the traditional Easter roast.

SERVES 6–8

175g/6 oz/1^1/$_2$ cups plain flour
25g/1 oz/2 tablespoons cocoa powder
25g/1 oz/2 tablespoons golden
   icing sugar
125g/4^1/$_2$ oz/1^1/$_4$ stick unsalted butter,
   chilled and diced
1 large free-range egg yolk

FOR THE FILLING
70g/2^1/$_2$ oz dark chocolate
   (50–60 per cent cocoa solids), grated
3 lemons, preferably unwaxed
4 large free-range eggs, beaten
150g/5^1/$_2$ oz/^{2}/$_3$ cup golden caster sugar
150ml/5 fl oz/^{2}/$_3$ cup double cream
golden icing sugar, to decorate

1 Butter a 23cm/9 in fluted springform flan tin. Sift the flour, cocoa powder and icing sugar into a food processor with a pinch of salt. Add the butter, and process briefly until blended, or rub in the mixture by hand. Mix the egg yolk and 2 tablespoons cold water and slowly add through the feeder tube, or add while stirring. Gather into a ball, wrap in clingfilm and chill for 1 hour.

2 Roll out the pastry to fit the prepared tin, and prick the base with a fork several times. Chill for at least 2 hours, preferably overnight.

3 Preheat the oven to 200°C/400°F/Gas 6. Fill the pastry case with foil and baking beans and bake blind for 15 minutes. Remove the foil and beans and continue to cook for 5 minutes, then remove from the oven. Reduce the temperature to 170°C/325°F/Gas 3.

4 While the pastry is hot, scatter the grated chocolate over the base. Leave to cool slightly.

5 Grate the lemons' zest into a bowl, then squeeze and strain the juice into the bowl. Add the beaten eggs, sugar and cream, and beat until thoroughly combined. Pour this mixture into the pastry case, and place in the oven, taking care that the filling does not spill.

6 Bake for 30–35 minutes until the filling is just set. Cool completely before sifting over a thin film of icing sugar.

TARTE TATIN

A serendipitous mistake occurred in a provincial French town in the autumn of 1898. Caroline and Stephanie Tatin had been running their eponymous hotel in Lamotte-Beuvron in the Sologne region since 1888 when their father, Jean, had died. Stephanie, the elder sister, was the cook (Caroline ran the hotel) and one of her specialities was a delicious *tarte aux pommes*. One busy morning, she was behind with her tasks and had no dessert ready for lunch. Seeing the apples already peeled and cut, however, she quickly buttered a tin, sprinkled in some sugar then threw in the apples and slammed it into the oven, forgetting the rather crucial matter of the pastry base. It was only the aroma of sweet caramel that made her remember about it. She quickly made some pastry, moulded it over the top and threw it back in the oven, not having time to consider the consequences. When she finally removed it, she decided simply to tip it upside down on to a platter because it was a failure anyway. And, lo, the tarte tatin was born.

Soon, the gastronome, Curnonsky, discovered the joys of the tarte tatin, travelling by train from Paris just to eat it at Hotel Tatin. Some years after the sisters' deaths, he introduced it to Parisian gourmets in 1926 under the name *Tarte des Demoiselles Tatin*. Rather unsurprisingly, given the obsessive attitude of many in France to food, there is now a *Confrèrie* or Brotherhood (Sisterhood?), charged with 'defending the tarte tatin and promoting its consumption'. They even have Ten Commandments, which must be adhered to. These include 'loving the tatin with all one's heart and all one's soul' and honouring Stephanie and Caroline as '*mères de ce monde*' – mothers of this world. And we thought the British had the monopoly on eccentricity.

To make tarte tatin (once you have paid homage at the shrine of the Demoiselles) you need very few ingredients, but quality is paramount – and the apples must be the correct type. The ones recommended by the Confrèrie are La Reinette or La Belle de Boskoop, but they also accept La Golden, La Granny Smith, La Braeburn and La Cox's Orange. I like to use the latter (without the 'La'). Never use cooking apples for tarte tatin, as they become a light, fluffy mush.

It is important to caramelise the apples well before the pastry disc goes on top and it is baked. You want a nicely dark golden-brown caramelly goo sticking to each and every apple wedge. But if, by any chance, once it is inverted it still does not look deeply golden and rich, then just pop it under the grill until seriously dark and sticky.

And don't forget that, should any recalcitrant bits stick to the pan as you invert, just patch it up before serving. Even the experts do repair jobs; I feel sure that Stephanie Tatin's first attempt could not have been an utter triumph. But then, I am not one of the Sisterhood.

SERVES 6–8

225g/8 oz/2 scant cups plain flour
25g/1 oz/2 tablespoons golden icing sugar
150g/5½ oz/1½ sticks unsalted butter,
    chilled and cubed
1 large free-range egg, beaten

FOR THE FILLING
60g/2¼ oz/½ stick unsalted butter
60g/2¼ oz/¼ cup golden caster sugar
about 1.25 kg/2 lb 12 oz (about 8–10)
    dessert apples, peeled, cored and cut into
    thick slices

1 Sift the flour, sugar and a pinch of salt into a food processor and add the butter. Process until it resembles breadcrumbs, then slowly add the egg. Process briefly until you have a fairly moist dough, adding a teaspoon or two of cold water if necessary. Alternatively, rub the butter into the dry ingredients and stir in the egg and water.

2 Wrap in clingfilm and chill for at least 1 hour. Bring the pastry back to room temperature before using.

3 Preheat the oven to 190°C/375°F/Gas 5. To make the filling, melt the butter over a low heat in a 26cm/10½ in tarte tatin dish or a heavy-based frying pan that can be safely used in the oven. Add the sugar, stirring constantly. Cook gently for at least 5 minutes, or until golden brown. (Don't worry if it separates.) Do not allow it to burn.

4 Remove from the heat, and place the apples on top, in concentric circles or just any old how. Roll out the pastry to a circle about 5cm/2 in larger than the dish. Place the pastry over the apples and carefully tuck the edges inside the pan to form the tart's sides once inverted.

5 Prick the pastry a couple of times, and bake for about 35 minutes until golden brown. Remove from the oven, and leave for 10 minutes. Run a knife around the edges of the pan to loosen. Place a serving plate on top and invert swiftly and deftly.

6 Serve warm with crème fraîche.

LINZERTORTE

This is one of the recipes I demonstrated in the summer of 1993 when I was Guest Chef at the Royal Highland Show. Four times a day for four days, I cooked four or five recipes for the eager crowds in a stylish marquee. Because June weather in Edinburgh is so variable, there was often background noise to shout over – such as the tent flapping noisily in an Arctic gale or heavy rain pounding down on the roof.

Ten years on, I demonstrated at the Folklife Festival at the Smithsonian Institute in Washington DC. The contrast in weather could not have been greater – we needed industrial fans to keep us vaguely cool in the field kitchen where the preparation was done. And we dreaded when it was time to put on the ovens, as the temperature outside was well over 100°F.

Both the Scottish and American crowds' response to the baking was exactly the same, however: 'Why can't we taste?' (Hygiene laws usually prevent demonstrators giving out tasters.) But this rule was not all bad – it meant plenty more for the hard-working staff, for friends passing by – or for the cook herself, of course!

SERVES 8

50g/1³/₄ oz/¹/₄ cup golden caster sugar

125g/4¹/₂ oz/1 cup ground almonds, or hazelnuts

125g/4¹/₂ oz/1 generous cup plain flour, sifted

¹/₄ teaspoon ground cinnamon

125g/4¹/₂ oz/1¹/₄ sticks unsalted butter, chilled and diced

grated zest of 1 large unwaxed lemon

1 large free-range egg yolk

juice of ¹/₂ large lemon

300g/10¹/₂ oz/1¹/₂ cups best quality raspberry jam, preferably home-made

golden icing sugar, for dusting

1 Mix together the sugar, almonds or hazelnuts, flour and cinnamon in a food processor. Add the butter and process until the mixture resembles breadcrumbs, or rub in the mixture by hand.

2 Add the lemon zest and a pinch of salt and mix very briefly. Add the egg yolk and lemon juice and mix until a dough is formed. Chill for at least 1 hour.

3 Preheat the oven to 180°C/350°F/Gas 4 and place a baking sheet inside. Grease and flour a 20cm/8 in fluted flan tin. Roll out two-thirds of the pastry and use it to line the tin. Chill for 20 minutes. Prick the base, then spread over the jam evenly.

4 Roll out the remaining pastry and cut into long strips. Arrange in a lattice over the jam (see page 61 for lattice instructions). Place on the baking sheet and bake for 35–40 minutes, until the pastry is crisp and golden (the baking sheet helps the base to cook, as it has not been pre-baked). While still warm, dust with icing sugar.

RHUBARB AND WHITE CHOCOLATE LATTICE TART

The combination of white chocolate and rhubarb is heavenly. The natural tartness of rhubarb works beautifully with the delightfully cloying sweetness of white chocolate, which also complements the sharpness of fruits such as cranberries or raspberries.

SERVES 8

225g/8 oz/2 scant cups plain flour, sifted
25g/1 oz/2 tablespoons golden caster sugar
115g/4 oz/1 stick unsalted butter, diced
1 large free-range egg
1 tablespoon double cream

FOR THE FILLING
750g/1 lb 10 oz young rhubarb, cleaned and chopped into 2.5cm/1in pieces
2 tablespoons freshly squeezed orange juice
50g/1¾ oz/¼ cup golden caster sugar
115g/4 oz good quality white chocolate, chopped

FOR THE GLAZE
1 tablespoon double cream
2 teaspoons golden caster sugar

1 Place the flour, sugar and butter in a food processor with a pinch of salt. Process until it resembles breadcrumbs, or rub in the mixture by hand. Mix together the egg and double cream, then slowly add this through the feeder tube, with the machine running, or add while stirring.

2 Gather the dough together with your hands, and knead for a few seconds to form a ball. Wrap in clingfilm and chill for at least 1 hour.

3 Butter a deep, fluted, springform 23cm/9 in flan tin. Roll out two-thirds of the pastry to fit the prepared tin. Prick the base all over with a fork. Roll out the remaining pastry to form a rectangle, about 20 × 28cm/8 × 11 in. Cut into eight long strips, using a fluted pastry cutter if you have one. Place the strips on a large plate and chill in the refrigerator, with the lined flan tin, for at least 2 hours and overnight if possible.

4 Preheat the oven to 190°C/375°F/Gas 5. Fill the pastry case with foil and baking beans, and bake blind for 10 minutes. Remove the foil and beans and cook for a further 5 minutes. Remove from the oven and cool for at least 15 minutes.

5 To make the filling, place the rhubarb, orange juice and sugar in a pan, and slowly bring to the boil, stirring occasionally. Once bubbling, cook for no more than 5 minutes, or until the rhubarb is just cooked but still firm; do not let it become mushy. Drain over a sieve, reserving the liquid. Put the reserved liquid in a small pan and boil for 3–4 minutes, or until you have about 1–1½ tablespoons left.

6 Sprinkle the white chocolate over the pastry base, then spoon the rhubarb on top. Drizzle over the reduced juices.

7 Remove the lattice strips from the refrigerator and place them on the tart, to form a lattice (see page 61 for lattice instructions). The strips will be brittle, so take care not to break them. Trim any ragged edges.

8 Using a pastry brush, brush the cream all over the pastry strips, then sprinkle the caster sugar over the top.

9 Bake for about 30 minutes, until the pastry is golden brown. Cool for 30 minutes before transferring to a serving plate and serving with whipped cream.

Traditional cakes

Taking a home-made cake as a present is even more thoughtful than giving the ubiquitous bottle of wine or box of chocolates. Rather like making up a little posy of freshly picked garden roses, it shows true care. And you probably will have some inkling of whether the recipient prefers a Madeira cake, moist and buttery, to a dark and sticky gingerbread. Cakes evoke feelings of nostalgia, since, as the eaters bite into a cherry cake, they recall – in the manner of Proust and his madeleines – a visit to their grandmother as a child; or a Victoria sandwich cake – filled with jam or buttercream – bought after waiting in a long queue at the village fête during the halcyon days of childhood summers.

Those lucky enough to have visited Australia might remember chocolatey, coconutty lamingtons – or Scandinavian *tosca* cake, a delicious sponge topped with buttery crunchy almonds. But, apart from the sentimentality and the consideration you have taken over making your gift, there is also a fairly good chance that you will be offered some of it yourself . . . not that that is the point, of course. But it is nonetheless a pleasant possibility ∎

VICTORIA SPONGE CAKE

There are endless versions of this classic cake but this is a good basic recipe that is also very versatile.

Traditionally, it is filled with raspberry jam, then the top sprinkled with caster sugar. But I usually add a layer of buttercream with the jam. Some prefer whipped cream and jam – remember to use a 'loose' jam – home-made strawberry often fits the bill, or one of the commercial French conserves – for easier spreading.

Never consider substituting margarine for butter – I know it seems a hassle taking time to soften a hard block of butter – although it takes seconds in the microwave on Medium (not High, which will simply melt it) – but the resulting flavour is incomparable.

Another lovely idea for this recipe is to make a Baked Alaska (see page 75, which uses half the basic mixture). I use one-half in the cake tin and bake the remaining batter as either 12 little mini-buns or 10 larger buns in paper cases, baking for about five minutes less at the same heat.

And finally, make the same basic recipe into lamingtons, Australia's national cake. Bake the sponge in a square cake tin, and then cut into small squares and dip each (using two forks) into a thick chocolate butter icing and then into a dish of desiccated coconut.

SERVES 8

175g/6 oz/1¾ sticks unsalted butter, softened

175g/6 oz/¾ cup golden caster sugar

3 large free-range eggs

175g/6 oz/1½ cups self-raising flour, sifted

1 Preheat the oven to 190°C/375°F/Gas 5, and butter and base line two 20cm/8 in sandwich tins.

2 Place the butter in a food mixer with the sugar and beat for at least 5 minutes until the mixture is pale and almost white. (There is a noticeable difference in colour from the start, from creamy yellow to almost white, or pure white if you are using white refined sugar.) Alternatively, place in a large bowl and beat well with a wooden spoon for 15–20 minutes.

3 Add the eggs one at a time, beating well after each addition. I also scrape down the sides of the bowl well, to ensure the eggs are all incorporated. Add a little of the flour if the mixture begins to curdle.

4 Gently fold in the flour, then divide the mixture between the prepared tins. Bake for 20–25 minutes or until springy and just firm to the touch.

5 Leave in the tins for 5 minutes, then turn the cakes out on to a wire rack. Leave until cold before filling.

BAKED ALASKA

This can be made the day before and kept in the freezer overnight before baking.

As for which flavour of ice cream, use whichever you like (vanilla is classic but chocolate, toffee or nut are also good), provided it is good quality. Serve either with a cold raspberry purée or hot chocolate sauce.

SERVES 8

1 × 20cm/8 in sponge (made from half the Victoria Sponge mixture, see page 74)

1 litre/1³/₄ pints/4 cups good quality ice cream, slightly softened

3 large free-range egg whites

¹/₄ teaspoon cream of tartar

175g/6 oz/³/₄ cup golden caster sugar

1 Place the sponge on an ovenproof plate. Top it with the ice cream, moulding it quickly to shape into a dome.

2 Meanwhile, whisk the egg whites with a pinch of salt until stiff, then add the cream of tartar. Gradually add the sugar and continue beating until the mixture is stiff and glossy.

3 Working quickly, spoon the egg whites over the ice cream to cover it completely, sealing well around the base. Using the tip of a spatula, make a few little peaks that will look good when tinged with brown.

4 Freeze at once until needed.

5 Remove from the freezer about 20 minutes before you are ready to serve, while heating the oven to 230°C/450°F/Gas 8. Bake for about 5 minutes until tinged with golden brown all over. Serve at once.

ANGEL CAKES

Also called fairy cakes or butterfly cakes, these were one of my mum's party treats. Dinky little sponge cakes with their tops cut off and stuck back on with butter icing, they then resembled angels' wings. But some might say they were butterfly wings. Whichever, they are heavenly little cakes that are – you hope – also lighter than light!

MAKES 12

125g/4$\frac{1}{2}$ oz/1$\frac{1}{4}$ stick unsalted butter, softened

125g/4$\frac{1}{2}$ oz/$\frac{1}{2}$ cup golden caster sugar

2 large free-range eggs

125g/4$\frac{1}{2}$ oz/1 generous cup self-raising flour, sifted

FOR THE BUTTER ICING

100g/3$\frac{1}{2}$ oz/1 stick unsalted butter, softened

200g/7 oz/1$\frac{2}{3}$ cups golden icing sugar, sifted, plus extra for dusting

1–2 tablespoons milk or orange juice

1 Preheat the oven to 190°C/375°F/Gas 5, and put 12 paper muffin cases into a bun tin.

2 Place the butter in a food mixer with the sugar and beat for at least 5 minutes until the mixture is pale and almost white. (There is a noticeable difference in colour from the start, from creamy yellow to almost white, or pure white if you are using white refined sugar.) Alternatively, place in a large bowl and beat well with a wooden spoon for 15–20 minutes.

3 Add the eggs one at a time, beating well after each addition. I also scrape down the sides of the bowl well, to ensure the eggs are all incorporated. Add a little of the flour if the mixture begins to curdle.

4 Gently fold in the flour, then divide the mixture between the muffin cases. Bake for 20 minutes until risen and golden, then cool completely on a wire rack.

5 To make the butter icing, beat the butter until smooth in a food mixer or use electric beaters. Gradually beat in the icing sugar and enough milk or juice to make a spreadable, fluffy consistency.

6 Cut a slice horizontally from the top of each cake and cut the slices in half. Spoon (or pipe) butter icing on to the top of each cake, then place the two half-slices vertically into the cream on top of each cake, to form angel wings. Dust with icing sugar . . . and think ethereal thoughts.

CHERRY CAKE

Most recipes for cherry cake advise rinsing off the cherries' syrupy coating and quartering them, so that they are lighter and do not sink into the cake. They also advise coating the cherries in flour to prevent sinking. But all I like to do is wash and dry the cherries – thoroughly – then instead of mixing into the cake batter, I layer the whole cherries on to the batter, just above the centre of the cake. This means that a nice big wedge of cake will have a big, whole cherry sitting all plump and round inside it. I prefer using the natural-coloured glacé cherries, as the red colouring is totally unnecessary. If, however, you want the old-fashioned look of a pillar-box-red-studded, moist, golden cake then go for the regular ones.

MAKES 1

200g/7 oz/1½ cups natural-colour glacé
   cherries
175g/6 oz/1¾ sticks unsalted butter, softened
175g/6 oz/¾ cup golden caster sugar

3 medium free-range eggs
175g/6 oz/1½ cups self-raising flour, sifted
100g/3½ oz/¾ cup ground almonds
1–2 tablespoons freshly squeezed orange juice

1 Preheat the oven to 170°C/325°F/Gas 3, and butter and base line an 18cm/7 in round or square cake tin.

2 Rinse the cherries in a colander, then pat thoroughly dry on several sheets of kitchen paper; it is very important that they are completely dry, so do this well in advance, if possible, and keep patting them dry.

3 Beat the butter and sugar until light and fluffy – up to 5 minutes in a food mixer or 10 minutes by hand.

4 Add each egg one by one, stirring after each and adding a spoonful of the sifted flour after two, if it looks a little curdled. Gently fold in the flour and a pinch of salt, then the ground almonds and finally the orange juice, adding enough juice to make a soft but thick batter.

5 Spoon just over half the mixture into the prepared tin, then arrange the whole cherries over the top. Cover with the remaining batter, spreading gently out to level the surface.

6 Bake for about 1 hour for the square tin and 1 hour 20–25 minutes for the round tin, covering either tin loosely with foil for the last 10 minutes or so. Test by inserting a skewer into the centre: it should come out clean. The edges of the cake will also have shrunk slightly from the sides of the tin.

7 Remove the cake to a wire rack for 20–30 minutes, then run a knife around the edges and remove the cake. Leave on the rack to cool completely.

GERMAN APPLE CAKE

This is based on a recipe I was given during the three years we lived in the town of Willmund in Ost Friesland, North Germany. *Apfel Streusel Kuche* was served with tea (tea was drunk more in Ost Friesland than coffee) – and was also made with gooseberries, plums or rhubarb. This is a delicious cake that is good served cold with tea or coffee but almost better warm for pudding. For pudding, I like to serve it warm with tablet ice cream, which is made by gently stirring about 300g/10½ oz chopped tablet (Scots fudge) into a one-litre tub of best quality vanilla ice cream.

SERVES 6

100g/3½ oz/1 stick unsalted butter

100g/3½ oz/scant ½ cup golden granulated sugar

200g/7 oz/1¾ cups self-raising flour, sifted

1 large free-range egg

500g/1 lb 2 oz (about 3–4) cooking apples, peeled, cored and sliced

55g/2 oz/⅓ cup raisins

1 teaspoon ground cinnamon

55g/2 oz/¼ cup natural demerara sugar

1 Preheat the oven to 190°C/375°F/Gas 5 and butter an 18cm/7 in springform cake tin.

2 Melt the butter in a large bowl in the microwave or in a pan over a low heat.

3 Remove from the heat then stir in the granulated sugar, flour, egg and a pinch of salt. Mix together to form a stiff dough.

4 Place two-thirds of the dough into the base of the prepared tin, pressing out gently with your fingers to cover the base.

5 Mix together the apple slices, raisins, cinnamon and demerara sugar, then tip this into the tin, pressing down gently.

6 Place the remaining dough over the top in little clumps; I do this by tearing or roughly crumbling it between my fingers. Again, very lightly press down with your hands.

7 Bake for 1 hour until golden brown and cooked through; cover lightly with foil for the last 10 minutes or so.

8 Cool in the tin for roughly 20 minutes then carefully transfer to a plate and serve warm or cold.

LITTLE STICKY GINGER CAKES

These can be made in various shapes and sizes; my preference is little quarter-pound loaf tins, which look so cute when iced and served up. Or you can make two slightly larger tins – one to freeze, one to eat now. Or one large cake that can be made a couple of days in advance and iced on the day – then served up for a crowd. Whichever – they are all delicious!

SERVES 10–12

200g/7 oz/2 sticks unsalted butter

175g/6 oz/1 scant cup unrefined
   molasses sugar

2 tablespoons golden syrup

2 large free-range eggs

150ml/5 fl oz/$^2/_3$ cup milk

300g/10$^1/_2$ oz/2$^1/_2$ cups self-raising flour

2 teaspoons ground ginger

3 balls of stem ginger, drained from their
   syrup, chopped

FOR THE GINGER FUDGE ICING

300g/10$^1/_2$ oz/2$^1/_2$ cups golden icing
   sugar, sifted

140g/5 oz/1$^1/_2$ sticks unsalted butter,
   softened

4 tablespoons ginger syrup from the jar of
   stem ginger

2 teaspoons lemon juice

1 piece stem ginger, slivered, to decorate

1 Preheat the oven to 170°C/325°F/Gas 3. Butter and base line four mini-loaf tins (200g/7 oz each); or two 450g/1 lb loaf tins; or a 23cm/9 in square cake tin.

2 Place the butter, sugar and syrup in a pan and melt over a low heat. Stir, then cool for 10 minutes. Beat the eggs into the milk, then add this to the melted mixture. Sift the flour, ground ginger and a pinch of salt together in a bowl, add the stem ginger, then pour in the egg and milk mixture, combining gently yet thoroughly.

3 Tip this into your prepared tin(s) and bake for about 30 minutes for the mini loaf tins; about 50 minutes for the large loaf tins; or about 1 hour for the large square tin. Test by inserting a skewer into the centre: it should come out clean.

4 Remove and cool completely on a wire rack before removing from the tin(s).

5 To make the icing, beat the icing sugar, butter, ginger syrup and lemon juice together, then spread over the cake(s). Decorate with ginger slivers.

GINGERBREAD

This is a nicely moist, dark and dense gingerbread that keeps well. Add an extra teaspoon of ground ginger if you like a very gingery taste. This is also delicious warmed slightly and served with poached pears and clotted cream for pudding.

SERVES 8–10

100ml/3$\frac{1}{2}$ fl oz/scant $\frac{1}{2}$ cup milk

175g/6 oz/1$\frac{3}{4}$ sticks unsalted butter

175g/6 oz/1 scant cup dark muscovado sugar

3 tablespoons black treacle

325g/11$\frac{1}{2}$ oz/2$\frac{3}{4}$ cups plain flour

2 heaped teaspoons ground ginger

$\frac{1}{2}$ teaspoon mixed spice

1 heaped teaspoon bicarbonate of soda

1 large free-range egg

1 Preheat the oven to 150°C/300°F/Gas 2, and butter and line a 900g/2 lb loaf tin.

2 Place the milk, butter, sugar and treacle in a pan and place over a low heat, stirring, until melted.

3 Sift the flour, ginger, mixed spice and bicarbonate of soda into a large bowl with a pinch of salt.

4 Leave the melted mixture to cool for about 10 minutes, then beat the egg into it. Pour this into the flour mixture, stirring gently but thoroughly.

5 When well mixed, tip into the prepared tin, levelling off the surface. Bake for 65–75 minutes or until a skewer inserted into the centre comes out clean. Leave in the tin until cold, then invert on to a wire rack.

PARKIN

This has a completely different texture to regular gingerbread: it is crumbly and less moist – because of the oatmeal – yet by no means dry. Whereas I don't think gingerbread needs any embellishment, such as butter, this is good thickly spread with butter. It is traditionally associated with Bonfire Night in Yorkshire.

SERVES 12–16

100g/3½ oz/½ cup dark muscovado sugar

140g/5 oz/1½ sticks unsalted butter

3 tablespoons black treacle

150g/5½ oz/1¼ cups plain flour

1 teaspoon baking powder

¼ teaspoon bicarbonate of soda

2 teaspoons ground ginger

good pinch of ground mace

good pinch of ground cloves

200g/7 oz/1 generous cup medium oatmeal

1 medium free-range egg

50ml/2 fl oz/scant ¼ cup milk

1 Preheat the oven to 150°C/300°F/Gas 2, and butter and line a deep, square 23cm/9 in cake tin.

2 Place the sugar, butter and treacle in a pan and melt over a low heat, stirring. Cool for 10 minutes or so.

3 In a bowl sift together the flour and baking powder with the bicarbonate of soda, ginger, mace, cloves and a pinch of salt. Add the oatmeal.

4 Whisk together the egg and milk and stir into the flour with the melted mixture. Once all combined, tip into the prepared tin, levelling the top. Bake for about 45 minutes or until a skewer inserted to the middle comes out clean.

5 Remove the tin to a wire rack, cool for about 20 minutes, then carefully turn out the cake to cool completely.

NEW YORK CHEESECAKE

I prefer to use light cream cheese for this recipe: normally I eschew all 'low-fat', 'low-cal' etc. options but in this case, the light version does make this dense creamy cheesecake just slightly less rich, which means I can opt for my hefty generous slab instead of a dainty sliver.

Try to remember to make this the day before serving, to give it a chance to firm up. It will also decant from the tin more easily. If you can, leave in the oven overnight to ensure a crack-free surface. Should any of the biscuit crumbs be left on the tin once decanted, do not despair – sprinkle them purposefully over the top of the cheesecake for an impromptu decoration.

Serve with either a sharp fruit purée of raspberries, blackcurrants or brambles (blackberries) or with fresh fruit.

SERVES 12

200g/7 oz digestive biscuits, crushed
70g/2½ oz/¾ stick unsalted butter, melted
1 kg/2 lb 4 oz cream cheese (I use Philadelphia Light)
200g/7 oz/1 scant cup golden caster sugar
1 rounded tablespoon plain flour, sifted

4 large free-range eggs
grated zest and juice of 1 unwaxed lemon
2 teaspoons pure vanilla essence or pure vanilla-bean paste
150ml/5 fl oz soured cream

1 Preheat the oven to 180°C/350°F/Gas 4, and lightly butter a deep 24cm/9½ in springform cake tin.

2 Combine the biscuits and butter, and press into the base and a little way up the sides of the prepared tin. Chill for an hour or so.

3 Place the cream cheese, 175g/6 oz/¾ cup of the sugar and the flour in a food mixer and beat well until smooth. (Alternatively, place in a large bowl and beat using electric beaters.)

4 Add the eggs one at a time, beating after each addition. Then add the lemon zest and juice, and the vanilla. Once thoroughly combined, pour into the crust and bake for 15 minutes. Reduce the temperature to 150°C/300°F/Gas 2 and cook for a further 45 minutes.

5 Beat the sour cream and remaining sugar together. Remove the cheesecake from the oven and very carefully and slowly spoon the sour cream over the top, taking care not to break up the surface. Return to the oven to bake for a further 15 minutes, then switch off the oven but leave the cheesecake in for at least 1 hour (or overnight if possible).

6 Remove and allow to become completely cold before chilling then carefully removing from tin.

DANISH ALMOND CAKE

Based on the delicious Danish *toscakage*, similar to Sweden's *tosca kaka* – a buttery lemon sponge topped with crunchy almonds – this cake can be served with coffee or for pudding, with thick cream and seasonal berries.

SERVES 8–10

150g/5$\frac{1}{2}$ oz/1$\frac{1}{2}$ sticks unsalted butter, softened

150g/5$\frac{1}{2}$ oz/$\frac{2}{3}$ cup golden caster sugar

grated zest of 1 unwaxed lemon

2 large free-range eggs

100g/3$\frac{1}{2}$ oz/1 scant cup self-raising flour, sifted

FOR THE TOPPING

100g/3$\frac{1}{2}$ oz/1 stick unsalted butter

100g/3$\frac{1}{2}$ oz/$\frac{1}{2}$ cup golden granulated sugar

100g/3$\frac{1}{2}$ oz/1 cup chopped almonds

1 heaped tablespoon plain flour, sifted

2 tablespoons double cream

1 Preheat the oven to 170°C/325°F/Gas 3 and butter a 24cm/9$\frac{1}{2}$ in springform cake tin.

2 Cream together the butter and sugar with the lemon zest until light and fluffy. Gradually add the eggs, one at a time, beating well after each addition. Fold in the flour.

3 Tip into the prepared tin, smooth the top, then bake for 20 minutes until firm.

4 Meanwhile, make the topping: melt the butter in a small pan, then stir in the remaining ingredients. Just before the cake is cooked, bring the topping mixture to the boil. Remove the cake from the oven, pour the topping over the cake immediately, smoothing it out. Return to the oven and bake for a further 20 minutes, or until golden brown.

5 Remove to a wire rack and leave for 20–30 minutes to cool in the tin before carefully removing the cake. Serve warm.

CRUSTY LEMON CAKE

This is such a popular cake, as it is so moist and lemony with a lovely crunchy topping. It is also incredibly easy to make. The first three stages are: the mixing of all the ingredients, the baking, and the pouring of the topping (sugar and lemon juice) over the cake the minute it emerges from the oven. The final stage – waiting until cool enough to cut and eat – is the most difficult.

SERVES 8

175g/6 oz/1^3/$_4$ sticks unsalted butter, softened
175g/6 oz/^{3}/$_4$ cup golden caster sugar
the grated zest of 1 large unwaxed lemon
2 large free-range eggs
175g/6 oz/1^1/$_2$ cups self-raising flour, sifted

FOR THE TOPPING
the juice of 2 large lemons
100g/3^1/$_2$ oz/^{1}/$_2$ cup golden caster sugar

1 Preheat the oven to 180°C/350°F/Gas 4, and butter an 18cm/7 in square cake tin.

2 Cream the butter and sugar and lemon zest until pale and fluffy. Beat in the eggs one at a time, alternately with the flour and a pinch of salt.

3 Pour into the prepared tin, levelling the surface with a spoon. Bake for 25–30 minutes or until a skewer comes out clean.

4 While the cake is baking, mix together the juice and sugar for the topping. As soon as the cake is out of the oven, prick gently all over the surface with a wooden cocktail stick, and then very slowly pour over the topping, trying to ensure the surface is all covered.

5 Cool before cutting into squares, or remove the whole cake from the tin and place on a wire rack and serve whole.

TEA LOAF

This delicious, moist cake is based on my mum's Guggy cake, part of her regular tea-time repertoire. The original recipe, from just after the Second World War, contained lard, but I have replaced this with butter. There are no eggs in it, yet it is still wonderfully moist. Remember to start an hour or so earlier than usual, to allow time for the boiled mixture to cool. Serve in slices with or without butter.

MAKES 1 LOAF

150g/5$\frac{1}{2}$ oz/$\frac{3}{4}$ cup light muscovado sugar
150g/5$\frac{1}{2}$ oz/1 cup sultanas
150g/5$\frac{1}{2}$ oz/1 cup currants

125g/4$\frac{1}{2}$ oz/1$\frac{1}{4}$ sticks unsalted butter
2 teaspoons mixed spice
225g/8 oz/2 scant cups self-raising flour

1 Place the sugar, sultanas, currants, butter and mixed spice in a heavy pan with 250ml/9 fl oz/ 1 cup cold water. Heat gently until the butter is melted, then remove from the heat and allow to cool completely. Meanwhile, preheat the oven to 180°C/350°F/Gas 4, and butter and base line a 900g/2 lb loaf tin.

2 Once the sugar mixture is cold, sift in the flour and a pinch of salt, and combine well. Tip into the prepared tin, levelling the surface. Bake for about 1 hour or until a skewer inserted into the middle comes out clean.

3 Remove to a wire rack to cool completely in the tin before turning out.

MADEIRA CAKE

This is based more on an American pound cake (French *quart-quart*), rather than a classic Madeira cake, which has more flour than butter and sugar; this often tends to make it rather dry. I have added some grated lemon zest and juice for a subtle lemon tang. Although classically served with a glass of Madeira, I like to serve it either as it is, with tea – or as pudding: toast thick slices of the cake and serve with poached brambles (blackberries) or blueberries and a dollop of clotted cream or Greek yogurt.

An optional slice of candied lemon peel can be placed on top of the cake 10 minutes or so before it is removed from the oven.

This can also be converted into a seed cake – an old-fashioned English cake that traditionally used caraway seeds, which were also made into caraway 'comfits' (an aid to digestion) by coating the seeds with sugar – by adding one tablespoon caraway seeds instead of the grated lemon zest. Fennel seeds can also be used instead of the caraway.

SERVES 8

200g/7 oz/2 sticks unsalted butter, softened
200g/7 oz/1 scant cup golden caster sugar
grated zest of 1 medium unwaxed lemon

3 large free-range eggs
200g/7 oz/1^3/$_4$ cups self-raising flour, sifted
juice of 1 medium unwaxed lemon

1 Preheat the oven to 170°C/325°F/Gas 3, and butter and base line a 900g/2 lb loaf tin.

2 Cream the butter and sugar together until light and fluffy, then stir in the lemon zest.

3 Stir in one egg, about a third of the flour and a pinch of salt. Once well combined, add another egg, and another third of the flour. Finally add the last egg and the remainder of the flour. Stir well in between each addition and add the next egg only when the ingredients are well incorporated.

4 When everything is thoroughly mixed and smooth, add the lemon juice and combine well.

5 Spoon into the prepared tin, smoothing the top. Bake for 45 minutes, then lightly cover the top with foil and continue to cook until a skewer comes out clean – another 15–20 minutes.

6 Remove and cool in the tin for 30 minutes or so, then remove from the tin and transfer to the wire rack to cool completely.

DUNDEE CAKE

As a Dundonian, I am exceedingly proud of Dundee cake. Its origins – according to David Goodfellow of Goodfellow and Steven (one of Scotland's best bakeries, established in Dundee in 1897) – are closely linked to the marmalade industry. The surplus of orange peel from Keiller's marmalade was used in Dundee cakes. A sign, therefore, of an authentic Dundee cake is the use of orange peel, not mixed peel. Unless you are a purist, however, mixed peel of good quality will still make a very fine cake. Many classic recipes use sweet sherry or brandy instead of whisky, but I personally prefer to use Scotland's own spirit.

SERVES 10

175g/6 oz/1$^3/_4$ sticks unsalted butter, softened

175g/6 oz/$^3/_4$ cup golden caster sugar

grated zest of 1 large orange

3 large free-range eggs

175g/6 oz/1$^1/_2$ cups plain flour, sifted

1 teaspoon baking powder

$^1/_2$ teaspoon mixed spice

115g/4 oz/$^3/_4$ cup currants

115g/4 oz/$^3/_4$ cup raisins

115g/4 oz/$^3/_4$ cup sultanas

55g/2 oz/$^1/_3$ cup chopped mixed peel

1 tablespoon whisky (preferably malt)

16–20 whole blanched almonds

1 Preheat the oven to 150°C/300°F/Gas 2, and butter and line an 18cm/7 in cake tin.

2 Cream the butter, sugar and orange zest until light and fluffy, then beat in the eggs one at a time. Add a little of the flour if the mixture starts to curdle.

3 Add the flour, baking powder, spice and a pinch of salt. Fold everything together gently, then stir in the dried fruits and mixed peel, with the whisky.

4 Spoon into the prepared tin, levelling the top. Bake for 1$^1/_2$ hours, then remove and arrange the almonds on top in two circles. Return to the oven and continue to bake for a further 45–60 minutes (2$^1/_4$–2$^1/_2$ hours altogether).

5 Remove and cool completely before removing from the tin.

Modern cakes

Cakes are not just for tea-time. Charming though they are with a cup of tea mid-afternoon, they are also ideal for pudding. And unlike many hot puddings, which are best made shortly before dinner is served (and when you are in mid-flap), cakes can usually be made in advance and then reheated as appropriate to be served with ice cream, yogurt or cream – and perhaps a little spoonful of fresh or poached fruit. The less traditional cakes in this chapter can also be slightly messy, and so pudding bowls instead of dainty cake plates are de rigueur.

Cheesecake made with brownies and toffee or chocolate cake with meringue and lemon curd might not seem as sensible as, say, a Dundee cake or a seed cake, but that is their attraction. There is an air of mystery about serving up some new-fangled cake for pudding when guests perhaps expect a more classic apple crumble or steamed pud. But since it is the last thing your guests will eat, it is what they will remember. And what happy memories they will have. They will also wish they had had less of the main course so that they felt able to come back for seconds ∎

PASSION CAKE

This is one of those cakes that are terrific standbys if you are asked to bake a cake to take to a friend's birthday, school fête or church fair, as everyone loves it. I baked a large passion cake to take to my friend Mary-An's house the night before her wedding to be shared among her many Dutch relatives. As chief bridesmaid, I thought the wedding eve should also be memorable, and so a delicious cake was in order. My then two-year-old son Euan had helped me make the cake, and although I had been aware that when he was cracking the eggs into the cake a tiny piece of egg shell might have gone into the mixture, I had no idea that there was in fact a great deal of shell; although the cake was moist, it was also decidedly crunchy. Memorable indeed.

SERVES 8–10

250g/9 oz/2 cups self-raising flour, sifted

200g/7 oz/1 cup light muscovado sugar

1 teaspoon ground cinnamon

2 large free-range eggs

200ml/7 fl oz/1 scant cup sunflower oil

2 small bananas, mashed

125g/4$\frac{1}{2}$ oz finely grated carrot (this is the grated weight – you'll need 2 large carrots)

50g/1$\frac{3}{4}$ oz/$\frac{1}{3}$ cup desiccated coconut

50g/1$\frac{3}{4}$ oz/$\frac{1}{2}$ cup walnuts, chopped

50g/1$\frac{3}{4}$ oz/$\frac{1}{3}$ cup raisins

50g/1$\frac{3}{4}$ oz/$\frac{1}{2}$ cup macadamia nuts, chopped

FOR THE FILLING AND TOPPING

100g/3$\frac{1}{2}$ oz/1 stick unsalted butter, softened

100g/3$\frac{1}{2}$ oz cream cheese (I use Philadelphia Light)

2 teaspoons vanilla extract

250g/9 oz/2 cups golden icing sugar, sifted

1 tablespoon walnuts, chopped

1 Preheat the oven to 180°C/350°F/Gas 4, and lightly butter two 20cm/8 in sandwich tins.

2 Mix the flour, sugar and cinnamon in a bowl, then gently stir in the eggs and oil. Gently fold in the bananas, carrot and coconut with the walnuts, raisins and nuts.

3 Divide between the prepared tins, smoothing the surface. Bake for 35 minutes or until a skewer inserted into the middle comes out clean.

4 Place the tins on a wire rack to cool for about 20 minutes, then carefully invert and leave the cakes to cool completely on the rack.

5 To make the filling and topping, place the butter, cream cheese and vanilla in a food mixer and beat until smooth. Add the icing sugar and beat again until smooth. Alternatively, beat madly by hand, until thick and smooth.

6 Use half the mixture to cover one half of the cake and place the other cake on top. Carefully spread the remaining icing on top. Scatter over the nuts.

DUCK EGG PAVLOVA WITH CHEESECAKE CREAM

Duck eggs are especially good in baking. Perhaps it's because of their higher proportion of yolk to white or perhaps because the yolks have a higher fat content than hens' eggs. Make a sponge with them and you will be amazed how light and moist it is. Brownies, too, are lighter and somehow richer made with duck eggs.

But it is duck egg whites that are even more of a revelation: they have more protein than hens' eggs. Use them in pavlovas and I promise you the meringue will never stick to the paper – and no, you don't need any new-fangled lining paper or anything more than a tiny smear of oil on the greaseproof paper. I have even done it without oil at all and still stick-free. A miracle!

The idea for this recipe is inspired by Linda Dick, a Borders farmer who supplies much of southern Scotland with duck eggs from her flock of happy Khaki Campbells. These are the epitome of free-range ducks, released from the barn in the morning, to graze – yes graze – with the sheep on the hills. As they waddle over the stream and up the hill, gaits reminiscent of Groucho Marx (but without the cigar), it seems somehow axiomatic that happy ducks mean good eggs mean good baking.

SERVES 8

3 duck egg whites
    (a regular duck egg weighs 70g/2¹⁄₂ oz)
175g/6 oz/³⁄₄ cup golden caster sugar

FOR THE CHEESECAKE CREAM
300g /10¹⁄₂ oz cream cheese (I use
    Philadelphia Light)

40g/1¹⁄₂ oz/¹⁄₄ cup golden caster sugar
1 teaspoon pure vanilla extract
grated zest of 1 unwaxed lemon
150ml/5 fl oz/³⁄₄ cup whipping cream,
    lightly whipped
350g/12 oz/2 cups mixed berries
    (I like blueberries and raspberries)

1 Preheat the oven to 140°C/275°F/Gas 1. Lightly oil a sheet of greaseproof paper and place it on a baking sheet.

2 Whisk the egg whites with a pinch of salt until stiff (this takes longer than regular hens' eggs, but keep at it). Once they are at the stiff-peak stage, gradually add the sugar, whisking all the time.

3 Spread the mixture on to the greaseproof paper into a circle about 25cm/10 in diameter. Bake for 1¹⁄₂–1³⁄₄ hours, until set.

4 Remove from the oven and cool. Once cool, peel off the paper and set on a serving plate.

5 For the cheesecake cream, beat together the cheese, sugar, vanilla and lemon zest, then fold in the cream. Spread over the pavlova, then scatter over the berries.

CHOCOLATE MERINGUE CAKE

This is an unusual and utterly delicious cake based on a chocolate meringue cake recipe I wrote for my *Sunday Times* column in 1998 and it prompted the most readers' letters ever (mostly all good!). So I have adapted what was one large cake to make a sandwich cake with meringue crusts on top of each half and filled with a tangy lemon curd cream. It not only looks good, but it also tastes divine – and is perfect either for tea or as a dinner party dessert. If you prefer, you can omit the lemon curd cream and simply fill with whipped cream and perhaps some raspberries.

SERVES 6–8

115g/4 oz/1¼ sticks unsalted butter, slightly softened
115g/4 oz/½ cup golden caster sugar
3 large free-range egg yolks
55g/2 oz/½ cup cocoa powder
100g/3½ oz/1 scant cup self-raising flour
50ml/2 fl oz/scant ¼ cup milk

FOR THE MERINGUE
3 large free-range egg whites
¼ teaspoon cream of tartar
140g/5 oz/⅔ cup golden caster sugar

FOR THE LEMON CURD CREAM
2 heaped tablespoons lemon curd (preferably home-made, or use the Blackberry and Lemon Curd recipe on page 154)
200g/7 oz/1 cup crème fraîche

1 Preheat the oven to 170°C/325°F/Gas 3 and butter two 20cm/8 in sandwich tins.

2 Beat together the butter and sugar either by hand for 4–5 minutes or for 2–3 minutes using an electric beater; it should be light and fluffy.

3 Add the egg yolks, one at a time, beating well after each addition. Then gradually sift in the cocoa, flour and a pinch of salt. Pour in the milk and stir lightly until smooth. Spoon half the mixture into the prepared tins, smoothing down.

4 For the meringue, whisk the egg whites with a pinch of salt and the cream of tartar until soft peaks form, then gradually add the sugar and continue to whisk until thick and shiny.

5 Spoon the mixture over both cakes and bake for 20 minutes until the meringue is golden. Cool completely on a wire rack in the tins.

6 Remove from the tins and carefully place one cake, meringue-side up, on a serving plate. Beat together the lemon curd and crème fraîche and spread this over the top of the meringue. Top with the second cake, again meringue-side up. Either refrigerate or eat within a couple of hours.

CHOCOLATE COCA-COLA CAKE

This is a wonderfully moist rich chocolate cake. Inspired by a recipe in an American bake sale book, this version makes a fabulous birthday cake with its dark fudge chocolate icing. You will need almost one regular can of Coca-Cola for this recipe. And can I just add that I loathe Coke with a vengeance and seldom even allow it into the house, but have to admit it makes a truly excellent cake that everyone – adults and children alike – adores.

SERVES 10

250g/9 oz/2 cups self-raising flour
3 heaped tablespoons cocoa powder
$1/4$ teaspoon bicarbonate of soda
280g/10 oz/$1^1/4$ cups golden caster sugar
200g/7 oz/2 sticks unsalted butter
250ml/9 fl oz/1 generous cup Coca-Cola
100ml/$3^1/2$ fl oz/scant $1/2$ cup milk
2 large free-range eggs
1 teaspoon pure vanilla extract

FOR THE FROSTING

150g/$5^1/2$ oz/$1^1/2$ sticks unsalted butter
50ml/2 fl oz/scant $1/4$ cup Coca-Cola
3 heaped tablespoons cocoa powder, sifted
400g/14 oz/3 cups golden icing sugar

1 Preheat the oven to 180°C/350°F/Gas 4, and butter a 24cm/$9^1/2$ in springform cake tin.

2 Sift the flour, cocoa and bicarbonate of soda into a bowl, and stir in the caster sugar. Slowly melt the butter and Coca-Cola in a pan over a low heat. Add this slowly to the dry mixture, with the milk, eggs and vanilla, stirring all the time.

3 Once thoroughly (but gently) combined, tip the mixture into the prepared tin and bake for about 40 minutes, or until a skewer inserted into the middle comes out clean. Leave in the tin on a wire rack for about 10 minutes, then remove the sides of the tin. Cool on its base on the rack.

4 To make the frosting, slowly melt the butter with the Coca-Cola and cocoa in a pan over a low heat. Sift the icing sugar into a bowl, then pour the liquid over it, beating until smooth.

5 (If you want to save time, you can leave the cake in its tin for about 20 minutes, then transfer it to a serving plate. Carefully spread the frosting all over the top, then let it set for 10 minutes or so. Slowly release the sides. The icing will helpfully slide down the sides, to ice the cake fully. Convenient as this is, I find that, since the cake is still warm, some of the butter in the icing separates out a little, but this can be mopped up by lightly pressing some kitchen paper against it. Also, the cake is still sitting on the base of the tin, but if that doesn't bother you, then this is the quickest way to eat some delicious iced cake.)

6 If, however, you can wait, leave the cake until cold, remove to a plate then top with frosting.

CHOCOLATE SURPRISE CAKE

The surprise is the fact there is a whole jar of mayonnaise in this cake – a truly bizarre idea, you will be thinking. But pray consider what is in mayonnaise: eggs and oil, the combination of which happens to make a deliciously moist cake, which is precisely what this is. There is not even a hint of mayonnaise flavour – both in the raw mixture (well, I always live dangerously and lick the bowl, don't you?) and the finished cake.

Top with the fudge frosting used for the Chocolate Coca-Cola Cake opposite.

SERVES 10

250g/9 oz/2 cups self-raising flour

50g/1¾ oz/½ cup cocoa powder

¼ teaspoon baking powder

200g/7 oz/1 cup golden caster sugar

2 teaspoons pure vanilla extract

200g/7 oz good quality mayonnaise
(I use Hellmann's Real Mayonnaise)

1 medium free-range egg

1 Preheat the oven to 180°C/350°F/Gas 4, and butter and flour a 24cm/9½ in springform cake tin.

2 Sift the flour, cocoa and baking powder into a large bowl, then stir in the sugar and make a well in the centre. Add the vanilla, 150ml/5 fl oz/⅔ cup cold water, the mayonnaise and egg. Either beat with an electric hand-held beater (or with a wooden spoon) until it is smooth.

3 Spoon into the prepared tin and bake for about 30 minutes or until a skewer inserted into the middle comes out clean.

4 Cool on a wire rack, then remove the sides of the tin. Serve very slightly warm with berries and crème fraîche for pudding; or allow the cake to cool completely, remove the base, ice with fudge frosting and serve with tea.

GINGER LAYER CAKE WITH RHUBARB FOOL

This fabulous cake can be altered to suit the occasion – or indeed your mood. Should you want a rather sensible cake to serve for tea, just fill the middle of the cake with the fool. The remaining fool will keep in the refrigerator for another day to be served for pudding with shortbread. For an altogether more lavish cake that is more suited to pudding bowls than tea plates, spread the fool in the centre and also over the top, allowing it to drizzle down the sides. This effect also looks very alluring, but would not win prizes for decorating skills, for there is a definite air of reckless abandon about it. Either way it looks wonderful, with the treacly brown colour of the moist cake contrasting with the beautifully fabulous pink hue of the rhubarb. Once decorated or filled, the cake should be eaten on the same day. Only use young spring rhubarb, to avoid stringiness in later, older stalks and also to ensure a perfect pink.

SERVES 8

150ml/5 fl oz/$^2/_3$ cup light beer
175g/6 oz/1 scant cup dark muscovado sugar
$^1/_2$ teaspoon bicarbonate of soda
200g/7 oz/1$^3/_4$ cups self-raising flour
2 teaspoons ground ginger
2 large free-range eggs
100g/3$^1/_2$ oz/$^1/_2$ cup golden caster sugar
125ml/4 fl oz/generous $^1/_2$ cup sunflower oil

FOR THE RHUBARB FOOL

1kg/2 lb 4 oz young rhubarb, trimmed and
  chopped into chunks
2 tablespoons elderflower syrup
115g/4 oz/$^1/_2$ cup golden caster sugar
450ml/16 fl oz/2 cups whipping cream,
  lightly whipped

1 Preheat the oven to 180°C/350°F/Gas 4, and butter and base line two 20cm/8 in cake tins.

2 Place the beer and 125g/4$^1/_2$ oz/$^2/_3$ cup of the muscovado sugar in a pan and bring slowly to the boil. Remove from the heat and stir in the bicarbonate of soda. Leave to cool for about 1 hour.

3 Sift the flour and ginger into a bowl. Whisk together the eggs, remaining dark muscovado sugar, caster sugar and oil, then add slowly to the flour, stirring. Add the beer mixture and fold together gently. Tip into the prepared tins and bake for 25 minutes until just firm to the touch. Cool in tins for 30 minutes, then transfer to a wire rack to cool, peeling off the paper when cold.

4 To make the rhubarb fool, place the rhubarb in a pan with the elderflower syrup and sugar and bring slowly to the boil, stirring. Cook gently for 8–10 minutes until just tender. Allow to cool. Put the cream in a bowl, then gradually fold in the cooled rhubarb.

5 To serve, place one cake on a large serving plate and spread the fool generously all over. Place the other cake on top and serve now for couth tea. Or – for abandoned pudding – top with more fool so that it slithers down the sides and looks altogether too tempting for words. Devour with a good dessert wine while thanking the Good Lord for the seasonality of rhubarb.

CHOCOLATE BROWNIE AND TOFFEE CHEESECAKE

This is an outrageously rich, sticky cheesecake that even I, inveterate cheesecake lover, can only manage one slice of. Well, at the first sitting anyway.

SERVES 12

200g/7 oz digestive biscuits, crushed
70g/2$\frac{1}{2}$ oz/$\frac{3}{4}$ stick unsalted butter, melted
300g/10$\frac{1}{2}$ oz plain toffees
  (such as Thorntons original)
125ml/4 fl oz/generous $\frac{1}{2}$ cup milk
250g/9 oz (about 5) Dark Muscovado Brownies
  (see page 130)

600g/1 lb 5 oz cream cheese (I use
  Philadelphia Light)
140g/5 oz/$\frac{3}{4}$ cup light muscovado sugar
3 large free-range eggs
300g/10$\frac{1}{2}$ oz crème fraîche
2 teaspoons pure vanilla extract

1 Preheat the oven to 170°C/325°F/Gas 3, and lightly butter a 24cm/9$\frac{1}{2}$ in springform cake tin.

2 Combine the biscuits and butter and press into the base and a little way up the sides of the tin, then chill.

3 Put the toffees and milk in a heavy pan and place over a very low heat, stirring, until the toffees melt (about 5 minutes). Stir until smooth.

4 Meanwhile, tear the brownies into large chunks and scatter them over the base. Slowly pour the molten toffee over the top.

5 Beat the cream cheese and sugar together until smooth (I do this in a food mixer), then add the eggs, crème fraîche and vanilla. Continue beating until smooth.

6 Pour this mixture into the tin and place on a baking sheet (in case of leakage) in the oven. Bake for about 1 hour 10 minutes, or until there is still a tiny wobble in the middle when lightly shaken.

7 Remove and leave to cool, then remove the sides of the tin. Cool then chill. It is easier to remove from the tin the next day when completely cold.

BLUEBERRY POLENTA CRUNCH CAKE

An unusual yet moreish crunchy cake that is delicious served warm for pudding with thick cream or yogurt, or cold for tea.

SERVES 8

100g/3½ oz/½ cup, plus 2 teaspoons, polenta
250g/9 oz/2 cups self-raising flour, sifted
150g/5½ oz/²⁄₃ cup golden caster sugar
grated zest of 1 unwaxed lemon
150g/5½ oz/1½ sticks unsalted butter, diced

1 large free-range egg
1 tablespoon freshly squeezed lemon juice
200g/7 oz/1¼ cups blueberries
25g/1 oz/2 tablespoons natural demerara
  sugar

1 Preheat the oven to 180°C/350°F/Gas 4, and butter a 24cm/9½ in springform cake tin.

2 Place the 100g/3½ oz polenta, flour and sugar in a food processor with a pinch of salt and process for a few seconds. Add the lemon zest and butter, and process again until it resembles breadcrumbs. Alternatively, rub the lemon zest and butter into the dry ingredients by hand.

3 Add the egg and lemon juice then process, or mix, very briefly until just combined. Tip about two-thirds of this mixture into the prepared tin, pressing down all over.

4 Sprinkle the 2 teaspoons polenta over the base, then scatter over the blueberries. Sprinkle the demerara sugar over the top, then crumble the remaining mixture over to cover. Press down very lightly, and bake for about 35 minutes or until golden brown.

5 Cool on a wire rack for 20 minutes or so, then remove the sides of the tin. Serve warm or cold with thick yogurt or crème fraîche.

POPPYSEED AND LEMON MUFFINS

The combination of lemon and poppyseeds is excellent and one that I first came across in Sydney in the shape of dainty little friands: buttery two-bitesize cakes. I have adapted the recipe so that it can be made into either large muffins (ideal for breakfast or brunch) or dainty friands, which are ideal with tea.

MAKES 8 AMERICAN-STYLE LARGE MUFFINS, OR 14–16 FRIANDS

150g/5$\frac{1}{2}$ oz/$\frac{2}{3}$ cup golden caster sugar

150g/5$\frac{1}{2}$ oz/1$\frac{1}{4}$ cups self-raising flour, sifted

25g/1 oz/$\frac{1}{4}$ cup poppyseeds

grated zest and juice of 1 medium unwaxed lemon

125ml/4 fl oz/generous $\frac{1}{2}$ cup sunflower oil

2 large free-range eggs

1 Preheat the oven to 190°C/375°F/Gas 5. Put eight American-style muffin cases into a bun tin, or butter 14–16 mini-muffin or friand moulds.

2 Place the sugar, flour and poppyseeds in a bowl, then stir in the lemon zest. Make a well in the centre, then tip in the oil, eggs and lemon juice. Stir gently until combined.

3 Spoon into the muffin cases or moulds. Bake for 15–20 minutes for the friands or mini muffins, and 25 minutes for the large muffins.

DOUBLE CHOC-CHUNK CUP CAKES

These are best eaten warm so that the white and dark chocolates melt into the cake mixture. They not only look tempting when they are split open but they also taste delicious, with warm molten chocolate seeping into the light chocolate cake.

I prefer these un-iced but, if you like, decorate with a puddle of your own chocolate glacé icing. And don't buy chocolate chips for these. You need quality chocolate, which is best chopped by hand so that you will have chunks and not minuscule little chips.

MAKES 12 AMERICAN-STYLE LARGE MUFFINS

250g/9 oz/2 cups self-raising flour
50g/1¾ oz/½ cup cocoa powder
100g/3½ oz/½ cup light muscovado sugar
85g/3 oz/¾ stick unsalted butter, melted
200ml/7 fl oz/1 scant cup milk

2 large free-range eggs, beaten
2 teaspoons vanilla extract
115g/4 oz good quality dark and white chocolate, cut into chunks

1 Preheat the oven to 200°C/400°F/Gas 6, and put 12 American-style muffin cases in a bun tin.

2 Sift the flour, cocoa and a pinch of salt into a bowl. Beat together the sugar, melted butter, milk, eggs and vanilla. Pour slowly into the flour, while gently folding in the flour; do not over mix.

3 Gently fold in the chocolate chunks. Spoon into the muffin cases and bake for 20 minutes until risen and just firm to the touch.

4 Cool for at least 10 minutes on a wire rack before devouring warm.

WARM DATE CAKE WITH FUDGE TOPPING

This is reminiscent of sticky toffee pudding – and equally moreish!

It is one of the easiest cakes to make, as everything is mixed – cake and sauce – in the one pan. Serve in bowls, not plates, as the sauce is beautifully gooey, and because this is more pudding than cake, serve with a dollop of good ice cream (I like caramel or vanilla) or pouring cream.

SERVES 8

175g/6 oz/1 cup stoned dates, chopped
1 teaspoon bicarbonate of soda
85g/3 oz/^{3}/$_4$ stick unsalted butter, diced
85g/3 oz/^{1}/$_3$ cup golden caster sugar
70g/2^1/$_2$ oz/^{1}/$_3$ cup light muscovado sugar
175g/6 oz/1^1/$_2$ cups self raising flour, sifted
1 medium free-range egg, beaten

FOR THE FUDGE TOPPING
70g/2^1/$_2$ oz/^{3}/$_4$ stick unsalted butter
140g/5 oz/^{2}/$_3$ cup light muscovado sugar
100ml/3^1/$_2$ fl oz/scant ^{1}/$_2$ cup double cream

1 Preheat the oven to 180°C/350°F/Gas 4, and butter and base line a springform 18cm/7 in cake tin that is at least 10cm/4 in deep.

2 Place the dates in a large, heavy pan with the bicarbonate of soda and 250ml/9 fl oz/ 1 generous cup boiling water. Heat over a low heat for 4–5 minutes until the dates are softened. Remove from the heat and stir in the butter. Once it has melted, add the sugars and flour, and combine gently but thoroughly. Stir in the egg.

3 Pour into the prepared tin and bake for 25 minutes.

4 Meanwhile, place the topping ingredients in the same pan and bring slowly to the boil. Allow it to bubble away, stirring for 2–3 minutes.

5 When the cake has baked for 25 minutes, remove from the oven. Very slowly pour the sauce all over the top (it is important to pour slowly so that the cake does not suddenly collapse with a sudden surge of sauce). Carefully place back in the oven and continue to bake for 20 minutes until bubbling and risen.

6 Remove and cool in the tin for at least 1 hour, then carefully transfer to a serving plate to serve warm.

CITRUS RICOTTA CAKE

A moist tangy cake that is perfect served as dessert with some sliced mangoes or papaya, my recipe is based on talented cook Chris Stevenson's recipe, which she makes with lime zest. I first got to know Chris when she cooked and baked at Glass & Thomson in Edinburgh, one of my favourite 'Ladies Who Latte' cafés.

I like to use a mixture of lemon and orange, but try lime for an even tangier flavour.

SERVES 10

175g/6 oz/1^3/$_4$ sticks unsalted butter, softened

225g/8 oz/1 cup golden caster sugar

4 large free-range eggs, separated

175g/6 oz/1^1/$_2$ cups ground almonds

70g/2^1/$_2$ oz/^{1}/$_3$ cup fine polenta

1 teaspoon baking powder

grated zest of 3 unwaxed lemons and 1 small orange

250g/9 oz ricotta cheese

4 tablespoons freshly squeezed lemon juice

golden icing sugar, for dusting

mango slices, to serve

1 Preheat the oven to 150°C/300°F/Gas 2, and butter and base line a 24cm/9^1/$_2$ in cake tin.

2 Cream the butter and 175g/6 oz/^{3}/$_4$ cup of the sugar together until smooth. Beat in the egg yolks. Stir in the almonds, polenta, baking powder and the citrus zest and add a pinch of salt. Stir in the ricotta cheese and lemon juice, combining well but gently.

3 In a separate bowl, whisk the egg whites to the soft-peak stage, then fold in the remaining sugar. Gently fold this mixture into the polenta mixture, a little at a time.

4 Tip into the prepared tin, levelling the surface. Bake for about 45 minutes or until just set.

5 Remove to a wire rack and cover with a large bowl to keep in the moisture as it cools. Once cool, remove from tin, wrap in clingfilm and chill in the refrigerator overnight.

6 Dredge with icing sugar and serve in slices with the mangoes.

SPICED HONEY CAKE

The taste of this deliciously moist sticky spiced cake changes every time you make it, depending on which type of honey you use. My own preference is for a fragrant floral honey made from summer blossoms. Heather honey is really worth seeking out with its unusual gel-like texture.

The cake is my version of a Danish beekeeper's mother's recipe – given to me by the producer of my own favourite heather and blossom honeys, John Mellis, who has colonies of bees all over southern Scotland. In the original recipe, the cake is usually topped with a thick butter cream. I think it is so good – and so moist – it needs no further embellishment.

A final word: once you have got the T-shirt for standing nervously in a heather-lined glen in a beekeeper's 'moonsuit', with hundreds of bees swarming around inches from your face buzzing in unison, while watching the beekeeper (John) being stung even through his gloves as he removes the frames from the hives with the thick luscious honeycomb, you come to appreciate what a very special food honey is. Special, not only because beekeeping is a dangerous, time-consuming and arduous business but also because of the fabulous nuances of flavours from this 100 per cent natural food.

SERVES 12

2 large free-range eggs
115g/4 oz/$\frac{1}{2}$ cup light muscovado sugar
55g/2 oz/$\frac{1}{4}$ cup golden granulated sugar
250g/9 oz/1 cup clear honey
   (or gently warmed set honey)
300g/10$\frac{1}{2}$ oz/2$\frac{1}{2}$ cups plain flour

1 teaspoon bicarbonate of soda
125ml/4 fl oz/generous $\frac{1}{2}$ cup cold water
125ml/4 fl oz/generous $\frac{1}{2}$ cup cold
   black coffee
$\frac{1}{4}$ teaspoon ground cloves
1 teaspoon ground cinnamon

1 Preheat the oven to 180°C/350°F/Gas 4, and butter and line a 23cm/9 in square cake tin.

2 Mix the eggs with the muscovado sugar then stir into the remaining ingredients in this order (beating after each): granulated sugar, honey, flour and bicarbonate of soda sifted together, then add the cold water, coffee and spices.

3 Once well combined, tip into the prepared tin and bake for 45–50 minutes or until a skewer inserted into the middle comes out clean.

4 Leave to cool in the tin for 10 minutes, then carefully invert on to a wire rack to cool.

Biscuits and cookies

Everyone loves a biscuit. Some might protest they do not, but when offered a little something with their tea, who can refuse? When I used to stay at my aunt Muriel's home in Dundee, I was given an early morning cup of tea in bed and with that drink came a biscuit, usually a buttery piece of shortbread; just what was needed to gear the appetite up for the porridge and Arbroath smokies to follow.

And although my own children have always been the contrary sort who loved going to friends' houses where they could have such novelties as packet custard creams or wrapped chocolate biscuits, their friends seemed to enjoy the contents of our cookie jars filled with home-made goodies. The great thing about biscuits is that they keep well and so they can usually last up to a week. They are also eminently versatile, served with morning coffee, afternoon tea, sandwiched together with a scoop of ice cream for pudding or – for the savoury ones – served with a glass of chilled fino sherry or champagne. And let us not forget that Scots New Year classic, shortbread with a slice of Cheddar and a dram. Perhaps not to be recommended first thing in the morning, however ∎

CLASSIC CHOCOLATE CHIP COOKIE

This recipe is based on the classic American Toll House cookie, which was the original choc chip cookie. Dating from the early 1930s from the Toll House Inn, Massachusetts, it came about, rather like our own dear Bakewell tart, as a serendipitous discovery. Ruth Wakefield, who owned the restaurant, ran out of nuts to put in her famous Butter Drop-do's and so broke up a chocolate bar and added it instead. She expected the chocolate to melt into the cookies but the result was gooey little chunks of chocolate that perfectly complemented the buttery crunchy cookie: the choc chip cookie had arrived!

Although many American recipes have a mixture of butter and margarine or shortening, I prefer all butter for better taste and purity of flavour. Many have a mixture of regular sugar and brown sugar, which is my preference; some add a bit of corn syrup for a chewy inside – but to my mind the most chewy texture in a cookie is found in the Super-chewy Chocolate Chip Cookies made with oil on page 114.

And the perfect accompaniment to a warm, freshly baked cookie? Yes, a cup of tea or mug of milky latte is all very nice but a tall glass of ice-cold milk (fresh or buttermilk) adheres to the all-American theme and is also a perfect match.

MAKES 20–24

125g/4$\frac{1}{2}$ oz/1$\frac{1}{4}$ sticks unsalted butter, softened
70g/2$\frac{1}{2}$ oz/$\frac{1}{3}$ cup golden granulated sugar
50g/1$\frac{3}{4}$ oz/$\frac{1}{4}$ cup light muscovado sugar
$\frac{1}{2}$ teaspoon pure vanilla extract
1 medium free-range egg

150g/5$\frac{1}{2}$ oz/1$\frac{1}{4}$ cups plain flour
$\frac{1}{2}$ teaspoon bicarbonate of soda
$\frac{1}{4}$ teaspoon salt
150g/5$\frac{1}{2}$ oz chocolate chips or chunks (milk or dark)

1 Preheat the oven to 190°C/375°F/Gas 5, and lightly butter two baking sheets.

2 Beat the butter and sugars together with the vanilla until creamy (I do this in a food mixer). Beat in the egg, then gradually sift in the flour, bicarbonate of soda and salt. Once it is just combined (do not overwork), stir in the chocolate chips.

3 Spoon heaped teaspoonfuls (or dessertspoonfuls) on to the baking sheets, and bake for 9–11 minutes until pale golden and still slightly soft in the centre. (If you are baking two trays at once be sure to swap them over halfway through cooking.)

4 Leave for 1–2 minutes before removing the cookies carefully to a wire rack to cool.

Variations and tips

■ Substitute some oatmeal (not porridge oats) for the flour (one-third oatmeal, two-thirds flour) for a crunchy texture. Omit the chocolate chips and replace with raisins, for oatmeal raisin cookies.

■ Add a heaped tablespoon of wholenut unsalted peanut butter to the butter for peanut cookies.

■ Chopped nuts are popular — add about 115g/4 oz/1 cup to the basic recipe. Try roughly chopped pecans, walnuts or hazelnuts, preferably lightly toasted.

■ Use white chocolate chips and add some toasted chopped macadamia nuts.

■ Add a small, ripe, mashed banana and 40g/1^1/$_2$ oz/^{1}/$_4$ cup chopped banana chips to the dough (just before adding the flour).

■ It is important not to overwork the cookie dough or the cookies will be tough.

■ Do not overcook the cookies or they will be all crunch and no chew.

■ Use either non-stick baking sheets or very lightly buttered baking sheets; too much butter will make the dough spread. An alternative is to line the baking sheet with baking parchment.

■ Once they are ready to come out of the oven (edges firm but centre gives a little when gently pressed with a finger) leave them on the baking sheets for 1–2 minutes; they are then less fragile and can be removed carefully to wire racks to cool.

SUPER-CHEWY CHOCOLATE CHIP COOKIES

These are truly chewy and soft inside yet nicely crisp outside – the perfect cookie, some may say – and they are certainly some of my family's favourites. They do not look as crisp or golden as regular cookies once ready to come out of the oven, but do not be put off – on cooling they attain that perfect balance between crunch and chew.

MAKES 20–24

175g/6 oz/1$\frac{1}{2}$ cups plain flour
$\frac{1}{2}$ teaspoon bicarbonate of soda
$\frac{1}{4}$ teaspoon salt
70g/2$\frac{1}{2}$ oz/$\frac{1}{3}$ cup light muscovado sugar
50g/1$\frac{3}{4}$ oz/$\frac{1}{4}$ cup golden caster sugar

125ml/4 fl oz/generous $\frac{1}{2}$ cup sunflower oil
1 medium free-range egg
$\frac{1}{2}$ teaspoon pure vanilla extract
150g/5$\frac{1}{2}$ oz chocolate chips or chunks
　(milk or dark)

1 Preheat the oven to 180°C/350°F/Gas 4 and lightly butter two baking sheets.

2 Sift the flour, bicarbonate of soda and salt into a bowl.

3 Beat together the sugars and oil until smooth using electric beaters, a food mixer, or beat by hand, then add the egg and vanilla. Gradually tip the flour mixture into the oil mixture and fold in gently. Stir in the chocolate chips.

4 Spoon heaped teaspoonfuls (or dessertspoonfuls) on to the prepared baking sheets and bake for 10–12 minutes until pale golden but still slightly soft in the centre.

5 Leave for 1–2 minutes on the sheets, then transfer carefully to a wire rack to cool.

CUSTARD CREAMS

There is a place on the east coast of Scotland that is worth travelling many miles to reach, if only to gaze upon the Glory that is the Cake Trolley. For in the But'n'Ben in Auchmithie, just north of Arbroath, you will find the most wonderful home-baking – towering scones, spicy cinnamon nablab, fluffy strawberry meringue cake, boozy coffee rum cake – all piled alluringly on to the shoulder-high cake trolley, which is trundled around the two tiny cottages that are joined together to form one of the most welcoming and unpretentious restaurants in the country. Margaret Horn has kindly shared her custard cream recipe with me and, although I have adapted it slightly, my version still tastes almost as good as Margaret's own. And it goes without saying, they taste a million times better than those packets of dreary, dusty custard creams that are two a penny on the supermarket shelves.

MAKES 8–10

200g/7 oz/2 sticks unsalted butter, softened
85g/3 oz/$^1/_3$ cup golden caster sugar
70g/2$^1/_2$ oz/$^2/_3$ cup custard powder
225g/8 oz/2 scant cups self-raising flour, sifted
a few drops pure vanilla extract

FOR THE BUTTER ICING
55g/2 oz/$^1/_2$ stick unsalted butter, softened
115g/4 oz/1 scant cup golden icing sugar, sifted
a few drops of pure vanilla extract

1 Preheat the oven to 180°C/350°F/Gas 4 and lightly butter two baking sheets.

2 Cream the butter and sugar together until smooth, then gradually blend in the custard powder, flour and vanilla extract. (I mix everything in my food mixer but it is easy by hand, well beaten with a wooden spoon.)

3 Using damp hands, roll into 16–20 small balls and place well apart on the prepared baking sheets. Using a fork dipped in flour, flatten each biscuit carefully, to give distinctive prong lines. Bake for 15–20 minutes (depending on the size) until a pale golden brown.

4 Remove to a wire rack to cool.

5 To make the icing, beat the butter until smooth, then add the icing sugar and vanilla extract. This will make a firm mixture. When the biscuits are cold, carefully sandwich two together with the icing filling to make 8 to 10 biscuit sandwiches.

SHORTBREAD

I am unashamedly proud of the fact that I was brought up on shortbread. Like so many other young Scots, a good piece of 'shortie' was a treat worth being good for – even worth enduring visits to deaf great-aunts or waiting in long queues at church fêtes. And in the halcyon days when everyone baked their own, there was as much talk about the difference between Mrs Kerr's and Miss McLeod's shortie as there is now between an oaked and unoaked chardonnay.

And with home-baked, there are plenty of differences in taste and texture, with so many factors contributing to memorable shortbread. First, there is the light touch. There is no use attempting shortbread if you have hot, eager fingers ready to knead rather than gently tease out your shortbread dough. Probably because many Scottish kitchens resemble freezers in winter, refrigerators in summer (or is that just mine?), the resulting cold hands could account for our light-fingered skills essential for shortbread, pastry and scones.

Then there are the ingredients: only the best will do. Never substitute margarine for the butter, since the whole point of shortbread is its buttery taste. A dough of all plain flour makes good shortbread but vary this by incorporating some rice flour (for a good crunchy texture), cornflour for a melt-in-the-mouth feel, or farola (fine semolina) for a texture between the two.

Variations on shortbread are endless – from modern-day Millionaire's Shortbread (with caramel and chocolate; see page 137) to old-fashioned Pitcaithly bannock (with almonds and peel), Tantallon cakes (with grated lemon) and of course petticoat tails, shaped in a segmented round with a small circle in the middle. And serving suggestions are also various: plain with tea, as pudding with a bowl of fresh berries and ice cream, or the Scottish Hogmanay classic – served with a wedge of cheese (I recommend Isle of Mull Cheddar).

MAKES 24–30

225g/8 oz/2$\frac{1}{4}$ sticks slightly salted butter, softened

100g/3$\frac{1}{2}$ oz/$\frac{1}{2}$ cup golden caster sugar, plus extra for dredging

225g/8 oz/2 scant cups plain flour

100g/3$\frac{1}{2}$ oz/1 scant cup cornflour, or farola or rice flour

1 Preheat the oven to 150°C/300°F/Gas 2. Lightly butter a 23 × 33cm/9 × 13 in Swiss roll tin.

2 Place the butter in a food mixer with the sugar and beat together until pale; this will take at least 3–5 minutes. Alternatively, beat by hand for double the time. Sift in the flours and process very briefly until the mixture is just brought together. Do not overprocess.

3 Tip into the prepared tin. Using floured hands, press down to level the surface. Prick all over with a fork, then bake for 45–50 minutes or until uniformly a pale golden brown.

4 Shake over some sugar from a dredger, then cut into squares or fingers. Leave for 5–10 minutes, then carefully remove to a wire rack to cool completely.

RASPBERRY SHORTBREAD

Based on Elizabeth David's raspberry shortbread from her *Summer Cooking,* this is less of a tea-time biscuit and more of a pudding, which is wonderful served with a dollop of Greek yogurt. In Mrs David's words, 'it is most excellent'.

SERVES 4

350g/12 oz/2$\frac{1}{2}$ cups raspberries
1 tablespoon golden caster sugar
125g/4$\frac{1}{2}$ oz/1 generous cup plain flour
55g/2 oz//1$\frac{1}{4}$ cup light muscovado sugar

good pinch ground cinnamon
$\frac{1}{2}$ teaspoon baking powder
55g/2 oz/$\frac{1}{2}$ stick unsalted butter, diced

1 Preheat the oven to 180°C/350°F/Gas 4. Place the berries in a shallow, ovenproof gratin dish. Sprinkle over the caster sugar.

2 Place the flour, muscovado sugar, cinnamon and baking powder in a bowl and rub in the butter until it resembles breadcrumbs. Spread this lightly over the berries, smoothing it out, but do not press down.

3 Bake for 25–30 minutes or until a pale golden brown. Serve warm or cold.

SHORTBREAD TOFFEE SANDWICHES

Based on Argentinian *alfajores*, these divine shortbread biscuits are sandwiched together with *dulce de leche* and then rolled in coconut.

I first discovered *alfajores* on a trip to Buenos Aires some five years ago to write about *dulce de leche*, that most wonderful thick toffee-like spread made simply by boiling up milk and sugar until golden and caramelised. In cafés in downtown Buenos Aires they are served with coffee – and in homes either home-baked or bought from bakeries to eat in the afternoon with tea or taken as gifts when visiting. In Argentina the shortbread rounds are often flavoured with lemon zest and/or cognac, and cornflour is always used as well as regular flour.

My Argentinian friend Mafe, who now lives in Edinburgh, tells me there are also *alfajores* covered in chocolate instead of coconut and also little pastries filled with *dulce de leche* called *canoncitos de dulce de leche*. For someone who, for midnight feasts as a camping Girl Guide, adored sucking condensed milk straight from a tube (they used to sell it in tubes like toothpaste), *dulce de leche* and any confections made from it are my idea of bliss. And before you ask, I still have all my teeth.

The shortbread rounds can also be served as they are, plain, with desserts such as poached fruit, creamy fruit fool or ice cream.

MAKES 25–30

250g/9 oz/2½ sticks unsalted butter, softened
140g/5 oz/1 generous cup golden icing sugar
1 teaspoon vanilla extract
200g/7 oz/1¾ cups self-raising flour
100g/3½ oz/¾ cup cornflour

FOR THE FILLING AND DECORATION
4–5 tablespoons *dulce de leche*
about 100g/3½ oz/½ cup desiccated coconut

1 Preheat the oven to 180°C/350°C/Gas 4. Place the butter in a bowl with the icing sugar and the vanilla and beat with electric beaters on a low speed for a couple of minutes until smooth. Sift in the flours and a pinch of salt and briefly beat on the lowest speed until combined.

2 With floured hands, bring the dough together. Wrap in clingfilm and chill for 30–45 minutes.

3 Roll out the dough until about 5mm/¼ in thick. Cut out 50–60 discs with a plain or fluted cutter (I prefer to use the smallest size of cutter) and place on unbuttered baking sheets. Bake for 10–12 minutes until lightly coloured (you may need to shuffle the trays around in the oven during baking, in which case allow a little longer).

4 Remove to a wire rack to cool. Once cold, very carefully spread one shortbread thinly with some *dulce de leche*, pushing it out to the edges, and top with another shortbread. Gently press together, taking care not to break the shortbreads, then roll the sides in coconut.

MERINGUES

Confession time: I have never really liked meringues. Apart from Baked Alaska (see page 75), where there is the obvious advantage – to me – of ice cream involved, they have never really done it for me. Perhaps because when I was a child the treat of a massive confection of two whiter-than-white meringues stuck together with often synthetic or tinned cream was never as appealing as, say, a freshly baked scone with butter and home-made jam. But now I realise that perhaps it was the very whiteness of the meringues that was the problem, for they tasted really of nothing, which is why I now make them only with unrefined sugar: golden caster for regular meringues that still have more flavour than refined-sugar ones; or, for a deliciously treacly edge, light muscovado sugar.

An alternative is to use half caster sugar, half icing sugar for a slightly more crumbly texture.

When making meringues, be sure to use eggs that are a few days old, and which are at room temperature. Duck egg whites make excellent meringues but need a little longer to whisk to stiff-peak stage.

MAKES 6–8

3 medium free-range egg whites

175g/6 oz/$^3/_4$ cup golden caster sugar or light muscovado sugar

1 Preheat the oven to 110°C/225°F/Gas $^1/_2$ and line a baking sheet with non-stick baking parchment.

2 Whisk the egg whites with a pinch of salt until stiff but not dry (it is meant to resemble cotton wool at this stage.) Very gradually add the sugar, beating well after each amount of sugar is added. Continue to whisk until it is shiny and stands in stiff peaks when you lift up the whisk.

3 Spoon out the mixture to make 6–8 blobs on the prepared baking sheet. Bake for 2 hours, then remove. Leave to cool.

4 Serve with whipped cream and fruit – or indeed with any ice cream dessert.

DIGGER BISCUITS

The recipe for these lovely crunchy biscuits was given to me by Christine Hall, mother of Linda Dick, the Borders farmer who raises the best chickens around. When I visited Christine at her own farm near Howgate in the Moorfoot Hills, she was preparing to cater the next day for 280 farmers and was cooking 44 kilos of beef to give them! Since these were Scottish farmers with their – our! – well-known sweet tooth, she had also spent days baking with her family. There was paradise cake, Annan biscuits, shortbread, fudge slice and digger biscuits.

Christine said her original recipe had come from an Australian relative, which makes sense, since diggers are very similar to those delicious Australian classics, Anzac biscuits.

MAKES 20

175g/6 oz/^{3}/$_4$ cup golden caster sugar

125g/4^1/$_2$ oz/1 generous cup self-raising flour, sifted

70g/2^1/$_2$ oz/^{1}/$_3$ cup porridge oats

40g/1^1/$_2$ oz/^{1}/$_4$ cup desiccated coconut

140g/5 oz/1^1/$_2$ sticks unsalted butter, softened

1 tablespoon black treacle

1 teaspoon bicarbonate of soda

1 Preheat the oven to 180°C/350°F/Gas 4 and lightly butter two baking sheets.

2 Place all the ingredients in a food processor and process briefly until well combined. Alternatively, mix by hand. Take small pieces of dough to form walnut-sized balls and place well apart on the prepared baking sheets. Flatten them a little by pressing down with the tines of a fork.

3 Bake for 15 minutes or until golden brown. They will feel soft when removed from the oven but will firm up on cooling. Leave for a couple of minutes, then remove to a wire rack to cool completely.

OVEN OATCAKES

Unlike traditional Scottish oatcakes, which are baked on a girdle (griddle) then finished off on a toasting stone in front of a fire, these are baked in the oven. Delicious eaten with cheese and celery, they are also good with honey. I particularly recommend them topped with a spoonful of sticky, crunchy honeycomb and then a sliver of farmhouse blue cheese such as Stilton or Dunsyre Blue. Rather like smoked salmon on rye bread, this is a match made in heaven. And all based on a simple oatcake.

MAKES 8

150g/5$\frac{1}{2}$ oz/$\frac{3}{4}$ cup medium oatmeal

70g/2$\frac{1}{2}$ oz/$\frac{2}{3}$ cup plain wholemeal flour

$\frac{3}{4}$ teaspoon baking powder

1 teaspoon golden caster sugar

$\frac{1}{2}$ teaspoon salt

50g/1$\frac{3}{4}$ oz/$\frac{1}{2}$ stick unsalted butter, diced

1 Preheat the oven to 170°C/325°F/Gas 3 and butter a baking sheet.

2 Place the oatmeal, flour, baking powder, sugar and salt in a bowl. Rub in the butter until it resembles breadcrumbs. Slowly add enough cold water (about 50ml/2 fl oz/$\frac{1}{4}$ cup) so that you can combine the mixture into a ball with your hands. Do not overwork.

3 Roll out gently to a 23cm/9 in round and cut into eight wedges. Transfer to the prepared baking sheet and bake for about 30 minutes or until the oatcakes have crisped up and are cooked through.

4 Transfer to a wire rack to cool.

PORRIDGE COOKIES

No, these are not made from the hacked-off slabs of porridge (taken from the porridge drawer) we all have to sustain us through those long winter nights in Scotland; they are simply cookies made with porridge oats. And I must say, they are some of the nicest cookies ever – really crunchy and oaty but wonderfully light. You can add a handful of chocolate chips or raisins to the basic dough for variety.

And incidentally, it is not fable about the porridge drawer – I have spoken to (elderly) people in Aberdeenshire who kept porridge in the drawer: vast pots of porridge were cooked then poured directly into the drawer of a kitchen dresser (called a 'kist' in the north-east) then allowed to solidify and cut into sections to take on the hills. And before you start the derisory comments, just think of north Italy's hip equivalent: cold polenta, made in the same way, cooled then cut into slices.

MAKES 18–20

200g/7 oz/2 sticks unsalted butter, softened
100g/3½ oz/½ cup golden caster sugar
150g/5½ oz/1 cup whole rolled (jumbo)
   porridge oats

85g/3 oz/¾ cup plain flour, sifted
¼ teaspoon bicarbonate of soda

1 Preheat the oven to 180°C/350°F/Gas 4 and grease two baking sheets.

2 Cream the butter and sugar together until smooth, then add the oats, flour, bicarbonate of soda and a pinch of salt. Stir until thoroughly combined.

3 Using floured hands, roll into 18–20 balls and place well apart on the prepared baking sheets. Bake for 15 minutes until golden brown.

4 Remove from oven, leave for 2–3 minutes, then transfer to a wire rack to cool completely.

ROCKY ROAD AND CHEAT'S FLORENTINES

Warning: this is one of the most moreish recipes in the book. I advise you not to make it at, say, 4 p.m., when blood sugar levels are down and you are desperate for a little something sweet with that cup of tea. Because once you start nibbling, it is tricky to stop.

The recipe is made on a baking tray divided roughly into two – one side with nuts and peel for adults (florentines), and the other with marshmallows and biscuits for kids (rocky road). Both sides are enrobed in best chocolate (opt for 70 per cent minimum cocoa solids for dark and minimum 30 per cent for milk) then broken up roughly into chunks. Since I find proper florentines rather a scutter to make, these cheat's ones are a million times easier and are made in a flash. The trouble is they also go in a flash.

MAKES ENOUGH FOR 10 ADULTS AND 10 CHILDREN

70g/2$\frac{1}{2}$ oz thick shortbread biscuits, roughly broken into chunks

70g/2$\frac{1}{2}$ oz mini-marshmallows

25g/1 oz (about 4) dried apricots, snipped

50g/1$\frac{3}{4}$ oz/$\frac{1}{3}$ cup macadamia or brazil nuts, roughly chopped

50g/1$\frac{3}{4}$ oz/$\frac{1}{3}$ cup whole almonds, roughly chopped

50g/1$\frac{3}{4}$ oz/$\frac{1}{3}$ cup chopped mixed peel

70g/2$\frac{1}{2}$ oz/$\frac{1}{2}$ cup dried cranberries or cherries

500g/1 lb 2 oz good quality milk and dark chocolate, combined

1 Place a sheet of baking parchment in a 23 × 33cm/9 × 13 in Swiss roll tin. Scatter the biscuit chunks, marshmallows and apricots evenly over one half of the tin. Scatter the macadamia or brazil nuts, almonds, mixed peel and cranberries or cherries over the other half.

2 Melt the chocolate in a heatproof bowl over a pan of hot water or in a microwave on Medium, then very slowly pour it over the top of the mixture in the tin. Smooth over the surface.

3 Chill, then, once set, cut up roughly into chunks.

CHEDDAR SHORTIES

These savoury shortbreads are delicious with drinks – or with a salad in summer or soup in winter. Use a mature farmhouse Cheddar, preferably unpasteurised for better depth of flavour.

MAKES 20

125g/4$\frac{1}{2}$ oz/1$\frac{1}{4}$ sticks unsalted butter, softened
150g/5$\frac{1}{2}$ oz/1$\frac{1}{4}$ cups plain flour, sifted
$\frac{1}{4}$ teaspoon salt

$\frac{1}{4}$ teaspoon ground cayenne pepper
125g/4$\frac{1}{2}$ oz/1 cup mature Cheddar cheese, finely grated

1 Preheat the oven to 150°C/300°F/Gas 2, and butter a 23cm/9 in square baking tin.

2 Place everything in a food processor and process briefly. Alternatively, rub the butter into the flour, salt and cayenne pepper by hand and stir in the cheese.

3 Tip into the prepared tin and press down to level the surface. Prick all over with a fork and bake for about 35 minutes or until pale golden brown. Cut into squares or triangles while hot, leave in the tin for 5–10 minutes, then transfer to a wire rack to cool.

PARMESAN SHORTBREAD

Crisp savoury cheesy bites, these biscuits are elegant enough to serve as canapés or, made slightly larger (but not thicker or they will not crisp up) they are also good with soup instead of bread.

MAKES 30

85g/3 oz/$\frac{1}{2}$ cup freshly grated Parmesan cheese
85g/3 oz/$\frac{3}{4}$ stick unsalted butter, softened

85g/3 oz/$\frac{3}{4}$ cup plain flour, sifted
$\frac{1}{4}$ teaspoon salt
1–2 teaspoons olive oil

1 Preheat the oven to 150°C/300°F/Gas 2, and butter a baking sheet.

2 Place the Parmesan, butter, flour and salt in a food processor and process briefly. Add enough oil through the feeder tube so that when you stop the machine it comes together in your hands to form a ball. Or, rub the butter into the dry ingredients by hand and stir in the oil.

3 Place on a sheet of clingfilm, roll into a 23cm/9 in long sausage shape, and chill in the refrigerator for an hour until firm. Using a sharp knife, cut into about 30 thin slices and place on the baking sheet. Prick each with a fork, then chill again for 10 minutes. Bake for 18–20 minutes until pale golden brown, then cool on a wire rack.

Brownies and bars

Traybakes and brownies are hugely popular; whether to be sold at school fairs or packed neatly into lunch boxes or picnic hampers, they are exceedingly tasty and deeply satisfying. And although my childhood was filled with such yummy treats as peppermint crumble bars, chocolate, cherry and coconut slice and millionaire's shortbread, I cannot but help feeling a little envious of today's youth who also have brownies. Of all the baked goods to have come across the Atlantic (some delicious: chocolate mayonnaise cake, Coca-Cola cake; some downright weird: tomato soup cake, potato crisp cookies), brownies are without doubt the best. As versatile as a Victoria sandwich cake (add nuts, apricots, marshmallows, berries; serve warm for pudding, cold with tea) and as easy to make as the proverbial apple pie (easier actually), they are now a staple, along with blondies and tiffin, of course. But brownies really are the best. If only they had been around when I was growing up. It's true what they say: kids today just don't realise how lucky they are ∎

DARK MUSCOVADO BROWNIES

This is, quite simply, the very best brownie recipe around – certainly according to my family. I bake these at least once a week, often more. Also, everyone outside the family who tries them ends up asking for the recipe, so that must say something about them. They are seriously chocolatey, wonderfully rich and squidgy, yet surprisingly light because of the low flour content.

Variations are endless: add 70g/2^1/$_2$ oz/^{2}/$_3$ cup chopped toasted walnuts or pecan nuts or chopped dried apricots to the batter. You can even bake it whole, as a brownie cake by first lining the brownie pan with greaseproof paper, lightly buttered, then, instead of cutting into squares, leave until completely cold before lifting out whole, ready to ice or decorate with whipped cream and fruit. Another idea is to cut the brownies into tiny squares for petits fours; it is easier to line the tin and chill the baked brownie completely before removing the entire lining paper and cutting.

Apart from serving with tea or coffee, freshly baked brownies, rather like freshly baked cookies, are also wonderful served with a glass of ice-cold milk. And finally, they are perfect for pudding, warmed slightly and served with a dollop of best ice cream and some fruit; I like raspberries, brambles (blackberries) or orange slices. A slug – or drizzle depending on who is in charge of the bottle – of crème de cassis, limoncello or Cointreau over the lot and you have a truly memorable pudding.

Regular 23cm/9 in cake tins that are both square and deep will do for this but since I have discovered a brownie pan with a slide-out base (see page 189) my brownie baking days are so much easier, as the entire base slides out, making cutting and removing them as easy as, well, eating them.

MAKES 16–20 BROWNIES

350 g /12 oz dark chocolate
    (55–70 per cent cocoa solids)
200g/7 oz/2 sticks unsalted butter
250g/9 oz/1^1/$_4$ cups dark muscovado sugar

3 large free-range eggs
70g/2^1/$_2$ oz/^{2}/$_3$ cup plain flour, sifted
1 teaspoon baking powder

1 Preheat the oven to 170°C/325°F/Gas 3 and butter a deep 23cm/9 in brownie pan or deep, square cake tin.

2 Melt the chocolate and butter together in a heatproof bowl over a pan of hot water or in a microwave on Medium, then stir until smooth.

3 Place the sugar in a bowl; if it is slightly lumpy, either break it up with your fingers or warm very slightly in the microwave (for a couple of turns) then stir it. Add the eggs one at a time, beating after each addition. Slowly add this to the melted chocolate mixture, stirring well.

4 Sift in the flour, baking powder and a pinch of salt and gently fold together. Tip into the prepared tin and bake for 35 minutes, or until a wooden cocktail stick inserted into the middle comes out with some moist crumbs adhering. It should also feel just firm when you place the palm of your hand gently on top.

5 Remove the tin to a wire rack and allow to cool for 30 minutes or so, then cut into 16 or 20 pieces. Leave until completely cold before removing the brownies.

BLONDIES

Blondies are brownies without the brown: natural blondes unlike brunette chocolate brownies. Moist little squares that taste strongly of the wonderful unrefined, light muscovado sugar, they are perfect for lunch boxes or tea-time. You can add some chopped pecan nuts if your consumers are nut-friendly.

A doddle to make, they are also very easy to devour straight from the wire rack, even before they have properly cooled.

MAKES 16

280g/10 oz/1$\frac{1}{3}$ cups light muscovado sugar
115g/4 oz/1$\frac{1}{4}$ sticks unsalted butter
2 large free-range eggs, beaten
175g/6 oz/1$\frac{1}{2}$ cups self-raising flour, sifted

2 teaspoons pure vanilla extract
100g/3$\frac{1}{2}$ oz/1 scant cup chopped pecan nuts (optional)

1 Preheat the oven to 180°C/350°F/Gas 4 and butter a deep 23cm/9 in square cake or brownie tin.

2 Melt the sugar and butter together (in a pan over a low heat or in a microwave), then stir.

3 Gradually add the eggs, beating all the time until smooth. Then sift in the flour and a pinch of salt. Add the vanilla and nuts, if using, and stir.

4 Tip into the prepared baking tin and bake for 25–30 minutes. Test after 25 minutes: the cake should be just firm all over when you lay your palm gently on top, and it will have a golden brown crust. A wooden cocktail stick inserted into the middle will emerge with a few moist crumbs, but no wet batter.

5 Remove the tin to a wire rack and leave for at least 30 minutes. Cut into squares and transfer to the rack to cool completely.

FRIDGE BROWNIES

So-called because these brownies are refrigerated before cutting, they are impossible to resist. Based on a wonderful recipe from my friend and fellow food writer Roz Denny, they are the gooiest brownies you can possibly imagine. As Roz says, the secret of the gooeyness is never to overcook and to allow them to firm and chill completely once cooked.

MAKES 20

200g/7 oz/2 sticks unsalted butter
200g/7 oz dark chocolate
   (minimum 60 per cent cocoa solids)
250g/9 oz/1¼ cups dark muscovado sugar
3 large free-range eggs

1 teaspoon pure vanilla extract
100g/3½ oz/1 scant cup plain flour
1 teaspoon baking powder
100g/3½ oz/²⁄₃ cup walnuts or
   dried apricots, chopped

1 Preheat the oven to 190°C/375°F/Gas 5, and lightly butter and base line a 23cm/9 in brownie tin with non-stick baking parchment.

2 Place the butter and chocolate in a heatproof bowl and melt over a pan of simmering water, or in the microwave, until melted. Stir well.

3 Beat together the sugar, eggs and vanilla until frothy. Beat the chocolate mixture into the sugar mixture, then sift in the flour, baking powder and a pinch of salt. Gently stir in the nuts or apricots.

4 Tip into the prepared tin and bake for 20 minutes, until a crust has formed.

5 Remove and cool for 2 hours, then chill in the refrigerator for at least another 2 hours before cutting and removing.

TOFFEE OATY SQUARES

These wonderful chewy toffee squares are basically an oaty base covered with a layer of toffee then topped with an oaty crumble. I recommend either Thorntons Original Toffees or Marks & Spencer Double Devon Butter Toffees.

MAKES 30

200g/7 oz/1$\frac{3}{4}$ cups plain flour

125g/4$\frac{1}{2}$ oz/$\frac{3}{4}$ cup porridge oats

150g/5$\frac{1}{2}$ oz/$\frac{3}{4}$ cup light muscovado sugar

$\frac{1}{2}$ teaspoon bicarbonate of soda

150g/5$\frac{1}{2}$ oz/1$\frac{1}{2}$ sticks unsalted butter, diced

150ml/5 fl oz/$\frac{2}{3}$ cup milk

200g/7 oz plain toffees

1 Preheat the oven to 180°C/350°F/Gas 4 and butter a 23 × 33cm/9 × 13 in Swiss roll tin.

2 Place the flour, oats, sugar and bicarbonate of soda in a food processor with a pinch of salt. Process briefly, then add the butter and process briefly again until the mixture starts to stick together. Alternatively, rub the butter into the dry ingredients by hand.

3 Press about three-quarters of this mixture into the prepared tin, spreading it out with your hands to form an even base.

4 Place the milk and toffees together in a pan and heat over a low heat, stirring until smooth (about 10 minutes), or in a microwave on Medium, stirring occasionally until melted.

5 Pour this slowly over the base, then sprinkle the remaining oat mixture over the top, rather like a crumble topping. Bake for 20 minutes or until the edges are golden brown.

6 Cut around the edges to loosen, then leave in the tin on a wire rack to cool completely before cutting into small squares.

BOUNTY BARS

A similar bar to the Chocolate, Cherry and Coconut slice on page 134, but uncooked and therefore quicker to prepare . . . just as quick to eat!

MAKES 30

350g/12 oz good quality milk chocolate (minimum 30 per cent cocoa solids)

100g/3½ oz/1 stick unsalted butter, softened

100g/3½ oz/¾ cup golden icing sugar, sifted

200g/7 oz condensed milk (half a regular can)

225g/8 oz/1¼ cups desiccated coconut

25g/1 oz quality dark chocolate, grated

1 Line a 23 × 33cm/9 × 13 in Swiss roll tin with foil.

2 Melt the milk chocolate in a heatproof bowl over a pan of hot water or in a microwave on Medium, then pour into the prepared tin and spread out to cover the base. Leave to harden.

3 Cream the butter and sugar together and stir in the condensed milk. Mix in the coconut, then spoon this mixture over the chocolate in the tin, spreading it out gently with a palette knife.

4 Scatter over the dark chocolate, then chill in the refrigerator until firm before cutting into bars.

MILLIONAIRE'S SHORTBREAD

This utterly delicious recipe is always a winner. And this recipe is now even better, I reckon, with Bill Plews's famous shortbread recipe as the base. Bill is the father-in-law of my dear friend Isabelle and whenever they come back to Edinburgh from their home in Zimbabwe, Bill bakes weekly batches of his lovely shortie, which disappear almost as soon as they are baked. So use the base as regular shortbread, too, for a change from my recipe on page 116.

If you cannot find *dulce de leche* (Argentinian toffee spread), boil up an unopened tin of condensed milk in simmering water for a couple of hours.

MAKES 24–30

450g/1 lb/4 cups plain flour, sifted
115g/4 oz/$^1/_2$ cup golden caster sugar
225g/8 oz/2$^1/_4$ sticks slightly salted butter,
    softened a little

FOR THE FILLING AND TOPPING
450g/1 lb jar of *dulce de leche*
250g/9 oz good quality milk
    or dark chocolate

1 Preheat the oven to 180°C/350°F/Gas 4, and lightly butter a 23 × 33cm/9 × 13 in Swiss roll tin.

2 Mix the flour and sugar in a large bowl. Add the butter, kneading gently in, to form a dough. (Bill does this by hand; I prefer to use a food mixer). Once it comes together in your hands, press it into the prepared tin, pressing down to level the top.

3 Prick all over with a fork and bake for 30–35 minutes or until pale golden all over. (Bill turns the tin around halfway through.) Remove (and if you are eating as shortbread, cut now into fingers). Cool the tin on a wire rack for about 30 minutes.

4 To make the filling, warm the *dulce de leche* by removing the lid and placing the jar in a microwave on Medium for a couple of minutes, until spoonable (or spoon into a pan and heat very gently.) Pour over the shortbread base, which will still be slightly warm. Leave to cool.

5 Melt the chocolate in a heatproof bowl over a pan of hot water and pour over the toffee, gently spreading out to cover. Leave to become completely cold before cutting into squares with a sharp knife and removing from the tin.

Quick bakes

Friends ring to say, 'We are in the area. Can we pop in?'

'Delighted!' So, since it's tea-time, you want to proffer not only tea but also a nice little something to eat. Instead of nipping off to the supermarket for a packet of dubious buns or biscuits, you decide to rustle up a batch of scones. Everyone likes a scone – however could you not? Oven on, ingredients weighed, a quick mix, and then patting out, cutting and on to the baking sheet. Once the oven is hot, whack them in. Ten minutes later they will emerge, just as the visitors arrive.

Smells of fresh, warm baking fill the house. A smear of butter and jam and you are not only giving your guests something delicious, you are perhaps making them also feel even more at home. You could have made damper (or Scotch pancakes, potato scones or Welsh cakes, which are even quicker, as they require no oven) and the result would have been the same: delighted tea-time guests. The trouble is, they will undoubtedly stay on for drinks, eagerly anticipating your fabulous little home-made canapés ■

SCONES

Scones are quintessentially British. I remember 'teaching' a Spanish gentleman sitting next to me on a shuttle flight from London to Edinburgh how to split open the scone in his afternoon tea tray then spread it thickly with clotted cream and jam; he had begun to eat the dry scone whole and was peering inquiringly at the cream and jam. What is blindingly obvious to us is perhaps not so to foreigners. Now, sadly, they serve only sandwiches on shuttles north and south.

MAKES 8–10

225g/8 oz/2 scant cups self-raising flour
1 teaspoon baking powder
2 teaspoons golden caster sugar

70g/2$\frac{1}{2}$ oz/$\frac{3}{4}$ stick unsalted butter, chilled and diced
150ml/5 fl oz/$\frac{2}{3}$ cup milk

1 Preheat the oven to 230°C/450°F/Gas 8 and lightly butter a baking sheet.

2 Sift the flour, baking powder and a pinch of salt into a bowl, then stir in the sugar.

3 Rub in the butter until it resembles breadcrumbs. Make a well in the centre and slowly add the milk, drawing the flour into the liquid with a table knife. Mix together gently. The dough should be soft but not sticky.

4 Bring the dough together gently with floured hands and tip on to a floured surface. Pat out gently to a thickness of about 2.5cm/1 in, then cut into scones using a fluted or plain cutter, or even an upturned tumbler. Place on the baking sheet and bake near the top of the oven for 12–15 minutes until risen and golden brown. Remove to a wire rack and eat barely warm.

Variations

- Substitute buttermilk for the milk (you will need about 200ml/7 fl oz/1 scant cup) for a moist, spongy scone.

- Add 40g/1$\frac{1}{2}$ oz/$\frac{1}{4}$ cup sultanas or currants to the dry ingredients. Or 40g/1$\frac{1}{2}$ oz/$\frac{1}{4}$ cup dark chocolate chips and the crushed seeds of 2–3 cardamom pods.

- My friend Hilary Wheeler's Coconut and Lemon Scones are delicious: mix 25g/1 oz/ 2 tablespoons desiccated coconut into the flour with the grated zest of 1 lemon and add an extra tablespoon or so of milk to bind. Bake as normal.

- For a savoury scone, mix 40–50g/1$\frac{1}{2}$–1$\frac{3}{4}$ oz/$\frac{1}{3}$–$\frac{1}{2}$ cup grated mature Cheddar cheese into the mix instead of the sugar. Top with a dollop of thick cheese sauce for a lovely crusty topping. Or snip 40g/1$\frac{1}{2}$ oz salami and a few basil or thyme leaves into a savoury scone mix.

AGA SCONES

The same rules apply with Aga scones as for regular scones: have a wettish, almost sticky mixture and handle as little and as lightly as you can. When baking scones in an Aga, they are even quicker to make than regular scones since, of course, the oven is already on. So all you need is, say, three to four minutes to prepare and 10 minutes to bake – quicker than going to the supermarket to buy dry, tasteless commercial ones . . . and a lot cheaper.

The final rule about scones is that they do not keep well, so eat on the same day – or freeze once cold. But they are seldom likely to last that long.

MAKES 6–8

225g/8 oz/2 scant cups self-raising flour

1 teaspoon baking powder

50g/1³⁄₄ oz/¹⁄₂ stick unsalted butter, chilled and diced

25g/1 oz/2 tablespoons golden caster sugar

175–200ml/6–7 fl oz/³⁄₄–1 cup milk

1 Butter a baking sheet. Sift the flour, baking powder and a pinch of salt into a bowl, then rub in the butter until it resembles breadcrumbs. Stir in the sugar, then add enough milk to make a fairly soft dough. Bring the dough together with floured hands and place on a floured surface. Pat out gently to a height of about 2cm/³⁄₄ in, then cut with a fluted or plain cutter into six to eight scones. Place on the baking sheet.

2 Slide the shelf on the third set of runners in the roasting oven and place the baking sheet on top. Bake for about 10 minutes or until just cooked. Remove to a wire rack to cool, then eat warm.

Scone tips

■ When making scones, use the lightest touch possible: if you knead vigorously, you develop the gluten and end up with a tough scone. Scone guru and craft baker Jimmy Burgess said his test for a light scone was to place one on the tip of an index finger – he says you should not be able to feel it, it will be so light. So remember, for scone-making, think happy thoughts (leave bad moods for bread-making).

■ All scones taste better warm, but do not eat them hot. They can be frozen on the day of baking then reheated in a loose foil parcel in a low oven.

■ Place 6–8 uncooked, sweet scones into an ovenproof dish of poached, sweetened fruit (blackberries, plums, rhubarb) and cook at 230°C/450°F/Gas 8 for about 20 minutes for a hot cobbler pudding. Serve it with cream.

TATTIE SCONES

These traditional Scottish flat potato scones are cooked on a girdle (griddle) or frying pan and are often served for breakfast or tea. You can add 25g/1 oz/2 tablespoons grated Cheddar to the mixture and serve them with a bowl of broth or lentil soup for lunch. Eat them warm, with a thin smear of butter, as soon after making as possible; leftovers can be toasted the next day.

Use a floury potato such as Maris Piper, King Edward or Pentland Dell.

MAKES 8

1 large potato (about 250g/9 oz)

25g/1 oz/$\frac{1}{4}$ stick unsalted butter

50g/1$\frac{3}{4}$ oz/$\frac{1}{2}$ cup plain flour

$\frac{1}{2}$ teaspoon salt

$\frac{1}{4}$ teaspoon baking powder

butter, for greasing

1 Peel and cut the potato into chunks, then cook in boiling water until tender. Drain well. Using a potato masher, mash the potato with the butter. Now weigh it: you will need 200g/7 oz.

2 Sift the flour, salt and baking powder into a bowl. While the mash is still warm, add the flour mixture and combine well. Using lightly floured hands, gently shape this mixture into two balls and turn on to a lightly floured surface. With a rolling pin, roll out gently to form two circles about 5mm/$\frac{1}{4}$ in thick. Cut each circle into quarters. Prick all over with a fork.

3 Heat a girdle (griddle) or heavy frying pan to medium-hot, smear over a little butter then, once hot, transfer four scones to it with a large spatula or fish slice. Cook for about 3–4 minutes on each side until golden brown. Transfer to a wire rack to cool briefly before spreading with a little butter and eating warm.

4 The tattie scones can also be made in advance; loosely wrap in foil and reheat in a low oven.

WELSH CAKES

Welsh cakes are traditionally cooked on a bakestone. Although this was originally a large slab of stone, heated up on a peat fire or a log, the bakestones now used are made of iron or some other heavy metal and are not placed on the fire, but on a gas or electric hotplate. As with all griddle cookery, a large, heavy frying pan will do instead, although it is less easy to maintain an even temperature. Like singin' hinnies from the north-east of England (which Welsh cakes resemble), there are many variations to this recipe: some have ground spices, such as nutmeg, mace, cinnamon or mixed spice; some have currants; some have a mixture of currants and sultanas, or even include lemon peel.

Their texture is short and soft, and the exterior almost crumbly. The cakes are often sprinkled with caster sugar immediately after they have been removed from the bakestone or griddle. They need no butter if eaten hot; once they are cold, however, a little butter or even jam would not go amiss.

If you have never made Welsh cakes before, the correct consistency of the dough is fairly light, but firmer and less soft than a scone dough.

MAKES ABOUT 12

225g/8 oz/2 scant cups self-raising flour

$\frac{1}{2}$ teaspoon mixed spice

$\frac{1}{4}$ teaspoon ground mace

115g/4 oz/1 stick unsalted butter, cubed

85g/3 oz/$\frac{1}{3}$ cup golden caster sugar

85g/3 oz/$\frac{1}{2}$ cup dried fruit (currants, sultanas)

1 medium free-range egg, beaten

about 1 tablespoon milk

golden caster sugar, to sprinkle (optional)

1 Sift the flour, spices and a pinch of salt together in a mixing bowl. Rub in the butter until it resembles breadcrumbs. Stir in the sugar and dried fruit.

2 Add the egg and just enough milk to form a light dough (firmer than a scone dough). Roll this out on a floured surface to a thickness of about 5mm/$\frac{1}{4}$ in. Using an 8cm/3$\frac{1}{4}$ in pastry cutter, cut out 12 rounds.

3 Lightly butter a bakestone or griddle, or heavy frying pan, and heat to medium hot. Cook the Welsh cakes, in two batches, for about 4–5 minutes on each side, until they are golden brown on both sides, but still soft in the middle. For a crunchy exterior, sprinkle with caster sugar immediately after cooking. Eat warm.

OVEN PANCAKE

During my year living in the north of Finland in the late 1970s, Thursday meant only one thing: thick pea soup and pancakes – these were usually oven pancakes with lingonberry jam. The Thursday ritual was a relic from medieval times when Friday fasting meant people ate substantial, pork-based pea soup to tide them over the following day's abstinence.

The soup–pancake duo is now often served in schools and also in the military, sometimes on Thursday but the actual day of the week is now more flexible; although it is also always served on Shrove Tuesday.

The pancake – called *Pannukakku* in Finnish – is a sweet Yorkshire pudding-like dish, which is served hot straight from the oven like a golden-crusted fluffy pillow, with a dollop of lingonberry or blueberry jam. A filling of sliced apples, lingonberries or blueberries can also be added to the base of the dish before adding the batter and baking in the oven.

I recommend you eat these after the pea soup from the Meat Pies recipe on page 44 as the combination of soup and pancake is perfect – and good for any day of the week.

SERVES 8

500ml/18 fl oz/2¼ cups milk

2 large free-range eggs

40g/1½ oz/3 tablespoons golden caster sugar

150g/5½ oz/1¼ cups plain flour, sifted

1 teaspoon crushed cardamom seeds (snip open a few green cardamom pods, remove the black seeds and crush them)

25g/1 oz/¼ stick unsalted butter

1 Place the milk, eggs and sugar in bowl and whisk together. Gradually incorporate the flour and crushed cardamom seeds, a little at a time, whisking until smooth.

2 Leave for 30 minutes, then whisk again. Meanwhile, preheat the oven to 220°C/425°F/Gas 7. Place the butter in a 28 × 18cm/11 × 7 in deep roasting tin and put inside the oven to heat.

3 Pour in the batter and return to the oven for 35 minutes, or until puffed up and golden brown. Serve cut into squares with a dollop of jam.

LEMON BERRY DAMPER

Damper bread is found increasingly in fashionable restaurants all over Australia, not simply in the bush, where it is traditionally cooked in the ashes of a campfire, in a camp 'oven' or twisted around green sticks over the fire.

A light scone-like bread, it can be varied by adding different flavourings. I particularly like the combination of lemon and blueberries.

Even if I buy fresh blueberries, I pop them into the freezer before combining with the dough, as fresh berries are so soft they tend to bleed into the mixture.

Serve warm – or at least freshly baked – with a tiny smear of butter.

SERVES 6–8

250g/9 oz/2 cups self-raising flour, sifted

55g/2 oz/¼ cup golden caster sugar

grated zest of 1 unwaxed lemon

1 medium free-range egg

75ml/2½ fl oz/⅓ cup sunflower oil

125ml/4 fl oz/½ cup milk

150g/5½ oz/1 cup blueberries
(preferably frozen)

1 Preheat the oven to 200°C/400°F/Gas 6 and butter a baking sheet.

2 Place the flour, sugar and lemon zest in a bowl, stir, then make a well in the centre. In another bowl, whisk together the egg, oil and milk, then add to the flour mixture. Using a knife, mix the dough together very quickly (overbeating will ruin the light texture). Very gently fold in the berries.

3 Tip the mixture directly on to the baking sheet and   using floured hands – shape lightly into a 20cm/8 in round. Score lightly into six wedges with a knife.

4 Bake for about 35 minutes or until tinged with golden brown and cooked through. Leave for a couple of minutes before transferring carefully to a wire rack to cool.

FLAPJACKS

I have included flapjacks in the Healthy chapter because oats are so terribly good for you, packed full of iron, zinc, vitamin B and soluble fibre. (I reckon that if we returned to the days of daily porridge instead of those sugary breakfast cereals, we would be a far healthier nation; we would also have more housekeeping money left over, as oats are so cheap.) For an even healthier recipe that is lower in fat, try the apricot and honey ones below.

It is important when baking flapjacks to remove them from the oven while they are still a little soft in the centre, as they harden during cooling. You can use a combination of whole rolled (jumbo) oats and porridge oats but do not use more than one-third whole rolled oats, otherwise the mixture is simply too crumbly to cut well.

MAKES 24

200g/7 oz/2 sticks unsalted butter
6 tablespoons golden syrup

450g/1 lb/2$\frac{1}{2}$ cups porridge oats

1 Preheat the oven to 180°C/350°F/Gas 4 and butter a 23 × 33cm/9 × 13 in Swiss roll tin.

2 Melt the butter and syrup together in a pan over a low heat or in a bowl in the microwave. Put the oats and a pinch of salt in a large bowl and add the butter mixture. Combine thoroughly.

3 Tip the mixture into the prepared tin, spreading it out so that the surface is even. Bake for about 25 minutes or until golden brown but still slightly soft.

4 Remove the tin to a wire rack, cut into squares or bars while hot, then allow to become completely cold before removing from the tin.

Variations

- Mincemeat Flapjacks: melt 175g/6 oz/1$\frac{3}{4}$ sticks unsalted butter with 6 tablespoons golden syrup and 200g/7 oz/1 cup good-quality mincemeat. Stir in 450g/1 lb/2$\frac{1}{2}$ cups oats, and proceed as normal.

- Apricot and Honey Flapjacks: melt 100g/3$\frac{1}{2}$ oz/1 stick unsalted butter with 85g/3 oz/ $\frac{1}{2}$ cup light muscovado sugar and 3 tablespoons honey. Stir in 350g/12 oz/2 cups oats, 100g/3$\frac{1}{2}$ oz/$\frac{2}{3}$ cup chopped dried apricots and 1 small mashed banana. Proceed as normal.

- Nutty Seedy Flapjacks: add 1 tablespoon each of chopped walnuts, chopped hazelnuts, pumpkin seeds and sunflower seeds to the basic mixture.

- Coconut Flapjacks: instead of 450g/1 lb oats, use 400g/14 oz/2$\frac{1}{4}$ cups oats and 55g/2 oz/ $\frac{1}{3}$ cup desiccated coconut.

BANANA FLAPJACKS

Chewy, moist and with a terrific banana hit, these oaty bars do, admittedly, have not only sugar but also a little syrup – but they are lower in both fat and sugar than normal flapjacks. And as we know, oats are super-healthy. I like to use mostly porridge oats but adding some whole rolled (jumbo) oats gives a more crunchy texture: about two-thirds porridge oats and one-third is a perfect ratio. If you use all jumbo oats the flapjacks tend to break up too easily.

MAKES 18–24

125g/4$\frac{1}{2}$ oz/1$\frac{1}{4}$ sticks unsalted butter
85g/3 oz/$\frac{1}{2}$ cup light muscovado sugar
2 tablespoons golden syrup

350g/12 oz/2 cups porridge oats
$\frac{1}{2}$ teaspoon baking powder
2 medium-sized ripe bananas, mashed

1 Preheat the oven to 180°C/350°F/Gas 4 and lightly butter a 23 × 33cm/9 × 13 in Swiss roll tin.

2 Melt the butter, sugar and syrup in a bowl in the microwave (or in a pan over a very low heat), then tip in the oats, baking powder and a pinch of salt. Once combined, stir into the bananas and combine well, then tip into the prepared tin, smoothing the surface with the back of a metal spoon.

3 Bake for 20–25 minutes, or until the edges are turning golden brown and it feels fairly firm all over.

4 Remove and cut into bars while hot, then leave in the tin until cold before transferring to a wire rack.

ROCK BUNS

These are not only a doddle to rustle up and bake, but they are also especially easy to eat. They are best served warm, straight from the oven, but if you want to bake them in advance, I recommend you freeze them, and thaw them on the day they are required.

Most recipes stipulate mixed peel as well as raisins or sultanas and currants, although I prefer just raisins and currants. But if you like, add 25g/1 oz/2 tablespoons peel and use only 125g/4$\frac{1}{2}$ oz/$\frac{3}{4}$ cup of other dried fruit.

MAKES 12

200g/7 oz/1$\frac{3}{4}$ cups self-raising flour, sifted
100g/3$\frac{1}{2}$ oz/1 stick unsalted butter, diced
150g/5$\frac{1}{2}$ oz/1 cup mixed dried fruit (raisins,
   currants, peel)

100g/3$\frac{1}{2}$ oz/$\frac{1}{2}$ cup natural demerara sugar
$\frac{1}{4}$ teaspoon ground ginger
1 medium free-range egg
4 tablespoons milk

1 Preheat the oven to 200°C/400°F/Gas 6 and lightly butter a baking sheet.

2 Place the flour in a bowl with a pinch of salt and rub in the butter. Stir in the dried fruit, sugar and ginger.

3 Mix the egg and milk together in a small bowl, then add to the fruit mixture and combine briefly to a stiff dough.

4 Pile into 12 rough little heaps on the baking sheet and bake for 12–15 minutes or until light golden brown. Eat warm or freshly baked.

APRICOT MUESLI MUFFINS

These muffins contain no sugar at all, just a little honey and some dried apricots for natural sweetness. Excellent for a wholesome breakfast.

Try to use organic apricots: although they might look rather unappealing with their dark wizened appearance, they are just as described on the packet – apricots that are harvested then dried in the sun, with nothing else added – and untreated with sulphur.

MAKES 12 AMERICAN-STYLE LARGE MUFFINS

140g/5 oz/1 cup dried apricots (preferably organic), chopped
grated zest and juice of 1 medium orange
200g/7 oz Greek yogurt (not low-fat yogurt)
115g/4 oz/1 stick unsalted butter, melted
3 heaped tablespoons clear honey
2 large free-range eggs, beaten

140g/5 oz/1^1/$_4$ cups self-raising flour
140g/5 oz/1^1/$_4$ cups wholemeal self-raising flour
1 teaspoon baking powder
85g/3 oz/^{1}/$_2$ cup Swiss-style, no-added-sugar muesli

1 Preheat the oven to 190°C/375°F/Gas 5 and place 12 American-style paper cases in a bun tin.

2 Soak the apricots in the orange zest and orange juice for about 20 minutes.

3 Combine the yogurt, butter, honey and eggs in a small bowl and stir into the apricot mixture.

4 In a separate bowl, sift together the flours and baking powder, add 55g/2 oz/^{1}/$_3$ cup of the muesli and add the apricot mixture, combining thoroughly but gently.

5 Spoon the mixture into the paper cases. Sprinkle over the remaining muesli and bake for 20 minutes until well risen. Eat warm.

MINI BLUEBERRY CRUMBLE MUFFINS

There is a most wonderful hotel in Sydney called The Observatory, situated in The Rocks area, a mere 10 minutes from Circular Quay and the Opera House. Apart from the many other reasons why this is such a special hotel (restorative spa, elegant rooms and unbelievably friendly staff), the breakfasts are splendid. So good, in fact, it is worth getting out of bed 20 minutes early to do a few lengths of the swimming pool, in order to arrive at breakfast utterly ravenous. As well as the tropical fruits, home-made muesli, bacon and eggs any which way, there are the pastries, all home-made. My favourites are pastry chef Stephan Kaptain's delicious blueberry crumble muffins. After three or four courses of fast-breaking, and feeling totally replete, I always manage to order yet another latte and return to the buffet table just one more time – to have a mini blueberry muffin. The trouble is, of course, stopping at one!

This is my adaptation of The Observatory's recipe.

MAKES 15

100g/3½ oz/1 stick unsalted butter, softened
100g/3½ oz/½ cup light muscovado sugar
1 large free-range egg
70g/2½ oz/²⁄₃ cup plain flour
70g/2½ oz/²⁄₃ cup wholemeal flour
1 heaped teaspoon baking powder
½ teaspoon cinnamon
50ml/2 fl oz/scant ¼ cup milk
150g/5½ oz/1 cup blueberries

FOR THE CRUMBLE TOPPING
70g/2½ oz/²⁄₃ cup plain flour, sifted
40g/1½ oz/¼ cup natural demerara sugar
40g/1½ oz/½ stick unsalted butter, softened

1 Preheat the oven to 190°C/375°F/Gas 5 and place 15 mini-muffin cases set in a mini-muffin tin.

2 Cream the butter and sugar together, then beat in the egg. Sift in the flours, baking powder, cinnamon and a pinch of salt, then stir in the milk. Now very, very gently fold in the blueberries, ensuring they do not burst. Use this mixture to fill the muffin cases.

3 To make the crumble, place the flour in a bowl, then stir in the sugar. Rub in the butter until it resembles breadcrumbs. Top each muffin with some crumble mixture, pressing down gently.

4 Bake for 20–25 minutes until golden brown and risen. Remove to a wire rack and eat warm or at room temperature . . . and I defy you to stop at one!

BANANA AND GRANOLA MUFFINS

Though you can, of course, cheat by using commercial granola, I do urge you to make some yourself. I used to make granola coated in ridiculous amounts of melted butter and, although it was delicious, it was hardly a healthy start to the day. But Turnberry Hotel chef, Colin Watson, gave me his superb recipe, which I have fiddled with a bit, but there is still very little fat for the amount of oats, nuts and seeds – all of which makes for a wonderfully healthy and delicious breakfast.

Although these muffins are lower in both sugar and oil than usual, they are nicely moist from the banana and also retain a good crunch from the granola. Perfect for breakfast, brunch or even afternoon tea.

MAKES 10 AMERICAN-STYLE LARGE MUFFINS

FOR THE GRANOLA
150g/5$\frac{1}{2}$ oz/$\frac{3}{4}$ cup whole rolled (jumbo) oats
50g/1$\frac{3}{4}$ oz/$\frac{1}{2}$ cup chopped walnuts
50g/1$\frac{3}{4}$ oz/$\frac{1}{3}$ cup whole unblanched almonds
50g/1$\frac{3}{4}$ oz/$\frac{1}{3}$ cup desiccated coconut
70g/2$\frac{1}{2}$ oz/$\frac{2}{3}$ cup sunflower seeds
100g/3$\frac{1}{2}$ oz/$\frac{3}{4}$ cup sesame seeds
2 tablespoons sunflower oil
2 tablespoons honey

FOR THE MUFFINS
150ml/5 fl oz/$\frac{2}{3}$ cup sunflower oil
2 large free-range eggs
115g/4 oz/$\frac{1}{2}$ cup light muscovado sugar
1 large ripe banana, mashed
150g/5$\frac{1}{2}$ oz/1 cup granola
$\frac{1}{4}$ teaspoon freshly grated nutmeg
200g/7 oz/1$\frac{3}{4}$ cups self-raising flour

1 To make the granola, preheat the oven to 150°C/300°F/Gas 2 and oil a baking sheet.

2 Place the oats, walnuts, almonds, coconut, sunflower seeds and sesame seeds in a bowl.

3 Put the oil and honey in a small pan and melt together over a low heat, then drizzle into the bowl, stirring well.

4 Spread thinly on to the baking sheet and bake for 25–30 minutes, stirring carefully a couple of times, until evenly browned. Do not allow the granola to go beyond golden brown. Remove and cool. Break up any large chunks and store in an airtight container.

5 To make the muffins, preheat the oven to 200°C/400°F/Gas 6 and place 10 American-style muffin cases in a bun tin.

6 Beat together the oil, eggs, sugar and banana, then stir in 100g/3$\frac{1}{2}$ oz/$\frac{3}{4}$ cup granola.

7 Sift in the nutmeg and flour and fold together gently.

8 Divide among the muffin cases and sprinkle 50g/1$\frac{3}{4}$ oz/$\frac{1}{4}$ cup granola over the tops. Bake for 20 minutes until risen and golden brown.

Festive baking

Special baking for festive occasions is not a prerequisite or the only way to ensure their success. But it certainly helps. Imagine a Christmas without cake or mince pies; or Easter without hot cross buns. There are, of course, far too many specialities from so many cultures and countries of the world to mention, but those given here are personal favourites: cakes, buns, muffins and pies – all completely different but all appropriate in their own way. In Sweden, 13 December would be nothing without its Lucia rolls, nor Christmas in France without its bûche de Noël. My childhood Christmases featured cloutie dumpling rather than cake – the former being the Dundee celebratory treat for birthdays and festive occasions. I compromise nowadays and serve dumpling for pudding, from my childhood, and cake later for tea, from my English husband's. The Irish barm brack reminds me of cloutie dumpling as there are coins hidden in the mixture, rather like the *galette des Rois* made for epiphany, with a ring inside – perfect for *Lord of the Rings* fans. Tuck one surreptitiously inside a large barm brack and serve for fans of the book and film, as I have done – and they will be happy as hobbits ∎

MINCE PIES

Good mince pies rely on two very obvious components: best mincemeat and light, buttery pastry. For the latter, I like to incorporate ground almonds into the shortcrust pasty to make it nicely crumbly and short. As for the mincemeat, if you have no home-made then buy the very best you can afford and tip it into a bowl. Stir in some finely chopped apricots, figs, almonds and hazelnuts, some grated orange zest and a good slug of brandy or Drambuie. But home-made is best both taste- and texture-wise.

I discovered a jar of home-made Drambuie mincemeat at the back of my larder and used it to make some delicious mince pies recently: the jar was at least five years old but the contents were still wonderfully moist and chunky. The only trouble was, the pies packed quite a punch, because although the mincemeat ingredients had blended together in perfect harmony over time, the effects of the alcohol content seemed to have doubled. If using well-matured mincemeat, do warn partakers that they might not be safe to drive afterwards.

MAKES 12

350g/12 oz/1⅓ cups luxury mincemeat, preferably home-made
200g/7 oz/1¾ cups plain flour, sifted
40g/1½ oz/3 tablespoons golden caster sugar

75g/2¾ oz/⅔ cup ground almonds
125g/4½ oz/1¼ sticks unsalted butter, diced
1 large free-range egg, beaten
milk, to glaze

1 Lightly butter a 12 hole pie or patty tin. Tip the mincemeat into a bowl and stir so that the liquid is evenly distributed. (If you are adding any extras, add them now.)

2 Place the flour, sugar, almonds and butter in a food processor and process briefly until resembling breadcrumbs, then slowly add the egg through the feeder tube. (Or rub the butter into the dry ingredients by hand and stir in the egg.)

3 Bring the mixture together with your hands, wrap in clingfilm and chill for an hour or so. Thinly roll out the pastry on a floured surface. Cut out 12 circles with a fluted pastry cutter, large enough to fill the base of the prepared tin. Press gently into each hole, then fill with the mincemeat.

4 Cut out another 12 slightly smaller discs and use to cover the mincemeat. Press the edges together to seal. Make a small slit in the top of each, then brush lightly with milk. Chill for about 30 minutes. Meanwhile, preheat the oven to 200°C/400°F/Gas 6.

5 Bake the pies for 20 minutes until golden brown. Remove to a wire rack and serve warm.

Variations

■ For chocolate and mincemeat tartlets, line 24 moulds, then fill with about 150g/5½ oz chopped good-quality dark chocolate before adding the mincemeat. Do not cover with a pastry lid. Bake at 190°C/375°F/Gas 5 for 18–20 minutes until the pastry case is golden.

■ For a crumble topping, sprinkle open tartlets with some of the Granola on page 168 and bake for about 2 minutes less.

■ Substitute ground hazelnuts for the ground almonds.

■ Once baked, carefully remove the pastry lid and insert a dollop of brandy butter or a sliver of Stilton cheese. Replace the lid then serve warm.

■ Dust the tops with sifted icing sugar while they are still warm to give a snow-scene effect if you like. (I personally think they are sweet enough.)

CHRISTMAS CAKE

This moist rich cake can be made well in advance: any time from the end of October (it keeps well for two to three months), but is best made at least four weeks before, so that every couple of weeks you can 'feed' it with brandy – even cakes get thirsty. Do not contemplate using a cheap brandy. Just consider all the expensive ingredients in there, so only the best will do for 'feeding'.

As for decorating, I confess I do not like the classic marzipan and royal icing topping on Christmas cake and so always finish with nutty topping, made by brushing warmed, sieved apricot jam on top, then sticking on whole nuts (brazils, walnuts, almonds and hazelnuts), preferably in neat rows. I then reglaze the tops with more melted jam. Tie a pretty Christmas cake ribbon around the sides of the cake and it will make a wonderful centrepiece on your sideboard beside the festive nuts, tangerines and chocolates.

SERVES ALL YOUR CHRISTMAS GUESTS

250g/9 oz/2$\frac{1}{4}$ cups self-raising flour

1$\frac{1}{2}$ teaspoons mixed spice

$\frac{1}{2}$ teaspoon ground cinnamon

$\frac{1}{4}$ teaspoon ground cloves

50g/1$\frac{3}{4}$ oz/$\frac{1}{2}$ cup ground almonds

350g/12 oz/2$\frac{1}{3}$ cups each raisins, currants
   and sultanas

50g/1$\frac{3}{4}$ oz/$\frac{1}{3}$ cup mixed peel

50g/1$\frac{3}{4}$ oz/$\frac{1}{3}$ cup dried apricots, chopped

50g/1$\frac{3}{4}$ oz/$\frac{1}{2}$ cup walnuts, roughly chopped

50g/1$\frac{3}{4}$ oz/$\frac{1}{2}$ cup whole (unblanched)
   almonds, roughly chopped

250g/9 oz/2$\frac{1}{2}$ sticks unsalted butter, softened

200g/7 oz/1 cup dark muscovado sugar

grated zest and juice of 1 unwaxed lemon

5 large free-range eggs

100ml/3$\frac{1}{2}$ fl oz/scant $\frac{1}{2}$ cup brandy
   (plus extra for feeding)

1 Preheat the oven to 150°C/300°F/Gas 2. Butter a 24cm/9$\frac{1}{2}$ in round, deep cake tin and line with a double layer of greaseproof paper so that it extends about 5cm/2 in above the rim.

2 Sift the flour, spices and almonds into a bowl, then add the raisins, currants, sultanas, mixed peel, dried apricots, nuts and a pinch of salt. Stir thoroughly. In a separate bowl, cream the butter, sugar and lemon zest until fluffy, then beat in the eggs, one by one, adding a teaspoon of the flour mixture with each egg. Stir the egg mixture into the flour mixture with the lemon juice and brandy.

3 Spoon into the prepared tin. Level the top and bake for 2 hours. Very loosely cover with a sheet of greaseproof paper and continue to bake for another 1 hour, making 3 hours in total, but test for readiness after 2$\frac{3}{4}$ hours' cooking. The cake is cooked when a skewer inserted into the middle comes out clean and the sides have begun to shrink from the edges of the tin.

4 Remove to a wire rack. Once completely cold, wrap in foil and store in an airtight container until Christmas, removing every 2 weeks to 'feed' (I make a diary note): unwrap, prick the top with a long skewer and spoon over 1–2 tablespoons brandy. Reseal as before.

MINCEMEAT CAKE

This gorgeous cake is moist and fruity, squidgy and crumbly. It is not only a doddle to make (sling everything in a bowl and mix), but it is also extremely versatile. It can be made a few days in advance – or on the day of serving. It works well as an alternative Christmas cake as it is altogether lighter – and is also very last-minute! It can be made specifically as a pudding: instead of allowing it to become completely cold, remove carefully to a serving plate while still just warm (do not attempt while piping hot or it will collapse) and serve in pudding bowls with a great scoop of best ice cream. Yum!

SERVES 8

175g/6 oz/1$\frac{1}{2}$ cups self-raising flour, sifted
150g/5$\frac{1}{2}$ oz/$\frac{3}{4}$ cup light muscovado sugar
100g/3$\frac{1}{2}$ oz/1 stick unsalted butter, softened
100ml/3$\frac{1}{2}$ fl oz/scant $\frac{1}{2}$ cup milk
200g/7 oz/1$\frac{1}{4}$ cups luxury mincemeat
   (buy the best quality; an inferior brand
   will ruin the cake)
2 medium free-range eggs
grated zest of 1 unwaxed lemon

FOR THE CRUMBLE TOPPING
200g/7 oz/$\frac{3}{4}$ cup luxury mincemeat
50g/1$\frac{3}{4}$ oz/$\frac{1}{4}$ cup light muscovado sugar
50g/1$\frac{3}{4}$ oz/$\frac{1}{4}$ cup whole rolled (jumbo) oats
$\frac{1}{2}$ teaspoon ground cinnamon
25g/1 oz/$\frac{1}{4}$ stick unsalted butter, melted

1 Preheat the oven to 180°C/350°F/Gas 4 and butter a deep, springform 18cm/7 in cake tin.

2 Place the flour, sugar and butter in a food mixer with the milk, mincemeat, eggs and lemon zest. Add a pinch of salt and mix on a low speed for a couple of minutes until thoroughly combined. Alternatively, mix with a wooden spoon. Tip into the prepared tin and bake for 30 minutes.

3 Meanwhile, mix the topping ingredients together in a bowl. Remove the cake and carefully sprinkle the crumble over the top with your fingers. Do it little by little, so that it does not sink into the cake. Return to the oven and continue to bake for a further 50 minutes or until a skewer inserted to the middle comes out clean (80 minutes baking altogether). Cover loosely with foil for the last 10 minutes or so to prevent burning.

4 Remove to a wire rack. Leave to cool for about 30 minutes before carefully removing the sides of the tin. Allow to cool completely and remove base if serving cold for tea, or eat barely warm if serving as pudding.

CHRISTMAS MINI-MUFFINS

These are delicious little two-bitesize muffins that are handy to bake in advance, and then freeze until ready to use. The two flavours are both festive and are delicious warm for tea instead of the ubiquitous mince pies.

You can substitute fresh cranberries for dried and although dried are so handy to have in the larder, the fresh berries with their natural tartness work extremely well with the cloying (yet alluring) sweet white chocolate. The cranberry/white chocolate muffins are more popular with children and the mincemeat/dark chocolate ones are popular with both children and adults.

I like to bake them in coloured foil containers for Christmas – gold, silver, green and red.

MAKES 24

200g/7 oz/1³/₄ cups self-raising flour, sifted
100g/3¹/₂ oz/²/₃ cup golden caster sugar
100ml/3¹/₂ fl oz/scant ¹/₂ cup sunflower oil
75ml/2¹/₂ fl oz/¹/₃ cup milk
1 large free-range egg

50g/1³/₄ oz good quality dark chocolate, chopped
1 heaped tablespoon luxury mincemeat
50g/1³/₄ oz good quality white chocolate, chopped
50g/1³/₄ oz/¹/₃ cup dried (or fresh) cranberries

1 Preheat the oven to 190°C/375°F/Gas 5, and put 24 mini-muffin cases inside a mini-muffin tin.

2 Mix the flour and sugar in a bowl, then make a well in the centre. Whisk together the oil, milk and egg, and slowly pour into the bowl, stirring gently. Divide this mixture between two bowls. In one bowl add the dark chocolate and mincemeat. Add the white chocolate and cranberries to the other bowl. Stir very gently.

3 Divide the two mixtures among the 24 muffin cases, and bake for 20 minutes or until golden brown and risen.

4 Remove the muffins to a wire rack and eat warm.

SUE LAWRENCE'S BOOK OF BAKING

ITALIAN CHRISTMAS CAKE WITH PINE NUTS

Inspired by a lovely Italian cake of chocolate, hazelnuts and walnuts by food writer Anna Del Conte, author of the fabulous *Gastronomy of Italy*, I have made a recipe with hazelnuts, pine nuts and chocolate and added a subtle almondy edge with some amaretti biscuits. It is delicious served barely warm with some whipped cream for pudding or at room temperature with tea as an alternative to our heavier traditional Christmas cake.

SERVES 10–12

extra virgin olive oil (mild not peppery)
50g/1¾ oz amaretti biscuits, crushed
300g/10½ oz/2 cups whole shelled hazelnuts
 (unblanched)
250g/9 oz quality dark chocolate
 (minimum 60 per cent cocoa solids),
 broken into small pieces

200g/7 oz/1 cup light muscovado sugar
4 tablespoons brandy
grated zest and juice of 1 large orange
100g/3½ oz/1 cup pine nuts, lightly toasted
6 large free-range eggs, separated
50g/1¾ oz/½ cup self-raising flour

1 Preheat the oven to 180°C/350°F/Gas 4. Lightly oil a deep, 24cm/9½ in springform cake tin with the olive oil.

2 Tip the crushed amaretti biscuits into the tin and swirl all around so the sides and base are coated with a fine dusting. Turn the tin upside down over a large mixing bowl to catch excess amaretti.

3 Place the hazelnuts and chocolate in a food processor and – using the pulse button – process on and off until you have a grainy consistency but not a fine paste (I need about 10–12 good blasts of the pulse button with my machine). Tip this into the amaretti bowl and add the sugar, brandy, orange zest and juice and pine nuts. Stir to combine, then add the egg yolks, stirring well. Sift over the flour, folding in gently.

4 Whisk the egg whites with a pinch of salt until stiff but not dry and gently fold this into the nutty mixture. Tip the mixture into the prepared tin and bake for about 1 hour or until a wooden skewer inserted into the middle comes out clean.

5 Remove to a wire rack and loosen off the sides of the tin. Allow to cool for an hour or so before carefully removing the base.

6 Eat at room temperate or slightly warm (so the chocolate melts a little).

BÛCHE DE NOËL

Unlike some bûches de Noël, or Christmas logs, this is not a dried-up old chocolate Swiss roll tarted up with a bit of icing made with margarine and refined icing sugar. The sponge base is light, mousse-like and moist. The filling can be either buttercream icing – all decorated with marshmallow mushrooms for the kids, if you like – and served for tea. Or serve it as a luscious sophisticated dessert, filled with cream and fruit. Whichever way, there will be compliments – and requests for seconds . . . and since it's Christmas, why ever not?

SERVES 8

150g/5$\frac{1}{2}$ oz/$\frac{2}{3}$ cup golden caster sugar

6 large free-range eggs, separated

250g/9 oz good quality dark chocolate
   (minimum 60 per cent cocoa solids)

FOR THE BUTTERCREAM ICING FILLING

250g/9 oz/2$\frac{1}{2}$ sticks unsalted butter, softened

450g/1 lb/3$\frac{2}{3}$ cups golden icing sugar, plus
   extra to decorate

50g/1$\frac{3}{4}$ oz/$\frac{1}{2}$ cup cocoa powder, sifted

2 tablespoons milk

FOR THE CREAM FILLING

400ml/14 fl oz/1$\frac{3}{4}$ cups double cream, lightly
   whipped

250g/9 oz/1$\frac{2}{3}$ cups raspberries

Drambuie (optional)

1 Preheat the oven to 220°C/425°F/Gas 7. Line a 23 × 33cm/9 × 13 in Swiss roll tin with greaseproof paper and brush this lightly with oil.

2 Combine the caster sugar and egg yolks in a bowl and whisk them together until light and thick. Melt the chocolate with 4 tablespoons cold water in a bowl over a pan of very gently simmering water. When you can see the chocolate has melted until smooth, stir in the sugar and egg mixture.

3 Meanwhile, whisk the egg whites until stiff but not dry. Gently fold a spoonful of the egg whites into the chocolate mixture to lighten it, then fold in the remaining whites using a large metal spoon. Do not overmix, and always use a gentle action. Pour the batter gently into the prepared tin and bake for 12–14 minutes (no longer), until risen and just firm to the touch.

4 Remove to a wire rack and leave to cool in the tin for at least 2 hours.

5 Once cold, lay a sheet of greaseproof paper on a board. With one bold movement, turn the whole cake on to the sheet of paper, then lift the tin off. Carefully peel away the paper and trim away any scraggy edges of cake.

6 To make the buttercream icing, beat the butter until soft then sift in the icing sugar and cocoa. Add the milk and combine together till soft. Spread half the icing over the cake up to the edges.

7 Roll up as you would a Swiss roll: starting at the long side opposite you, use the paper to roll the cake towards you, around the icing; don't worry about cracks. Transfer to a flat serving dish. Carefully spread the remaining icing over the cake (you can pipe the icing if you like – unless, like me, you believe life is too short). Chill until needed, then decorate with festive paraphernalia and finally sift over some icing sugar.

8 To make the cream filling, spread the inverted cake with the whipped cream, scatter over the berries and add a few dribbles of Drambuie, if you like. Carefully roll up as described above. Sift over icing sugar just before serving.

SWEDISH LUCIA ROLLS OR SAFFRON CAKE

On St Lucia Day (13 December) there are very particular customs that take place all over Sweden. Girls dress up in white, and one girl wears a towering crown of glowing lighted candles decorated with green cranberry leaves. They walk in a procession, singing Lucia songs, to celebrate the festival of light (the meaning of Lucia, from the Latin *lux*). The one wearing the candles is the Lucia, the other girls are called Tamor. Lucia rolls or buns (*Lussebullar* or *Lussekatter*) are baked for the festive period. These lovely little saffron rolls twisted into an 'S' shape are decorated with two raisins. The same mixture is often made into saffron bread in Sweden which takes the form of a plaited loaf decorated with rock sugar and flaked almonds.

But saffron bread is also very popular in Devon and Cornwall where it is called saffron cake. Although the basic mixture is similar to the one here, the dough is usually flavoured with dried fruit and peel, and sometimes clotted cream is added for extra richness.

I have tried various recipes for saffron bread but my one here is really moist and not too rich. The addition of quark ensures a tasty moistness; it was my Swedish friend Ingela Kassander who said that many of her friends incorporate some quark into their saffron bread dough, since some Lucia rolls tend to be dry. It is a clever trick and so, whether you make the rolls or a large loaf, the result is a saffron-flecked, moist bread that is all too easy to scoff, buttered or unbuttered. And don't feel you have to wait until December to bake this recipe.

MAKES 12 LUCIA ROLLS OR 1 SAFFRON CAKE

1 teaspoon saffron threads

250ml/9 fl oz/1 generous cup tepid milk (I use semi-skimmed)

500g/1 lb 2 oz/4$\frac{1}{3}$ cups strong white unbleached flour

7g/$\frac{1}{4}$ oz sachet of fast-action/easy-blend dried yeast

1 teaspoon salt

50g/1$\frac{3}{4}$ oz/$\frac{1}{4}$ cup golden caster sugar

50g/1$\frac{3}{4}$ oz/$\frac{1}{2}$ stick unsalted butter, melted

100g/3$\frac{1}{2}$ oz quark

1 medium free-range egg yolk

a handful of raisins for the Lucia rolls

1   If making the saffron cake, butter a 900g/2 lb loaf tin; if making the Lucia rolls, butter a baking sheet. Soak the saffron in the milk for 5–10 minutes.

2   Combine the flour, yeast, salt and sugar in a mixing bowl, and make a well in the centre. Stir the melted butter into the milk and saffron mixture and pour into the well.

3   Add the quark. Stir together, and then, using floured hands, combine to a dough. Knead on a floured surface for 10 minutes until smooth. Place in an oiled bowl, cover with oiled clingfilm and leave in a warm place for 1$\frac{1}{2}$–2 hours until well risen. Knock back the dough.

4   For the saffron cake: shape into a loaf and place in the prepared tin. Cover loosely with oiled clingfilm and leave in a warm place for 45–60 minutes until risen above the sides of the tin.

5   For the Lucia rolls, divide into 12 pieces and roll each into a rectangle about 20cm/8 in long. Twist each into an 'S' shape, as tight as possible. Place on the prepared baking sheet and cover loosely. Leave for 30–45 minutes or until puffed up.

6   Meanwhile, preheat the oven to 220°C/425°F/Gas 7.

7   For the rolls, brush with egg yolk, then place one raisin in the centre of each circle (two raisins per roll). For the cake, brush the top with egg yolk, taking care not to allow it to drip down the sides or it will stick to the tin.

8   Bake the rolls or cake for 15 minutes, then remove the rolls and place on a wire rack. For the cake, lower the heat to 200°C/400°F/Gas 6 and cover loosely with foil. Continue to bake for a further 20 minutes or until the cake sounds hollow when tapped underneath. Cool on a wire rack.

HOT CROSS BUNS

Traditionally, these buns are served on Good Friday, with the symbolic cross on the top. This is a really easy recipe that can be prepared in a flash. Then of course you have to leave the dough to rise twice, but that waiting time somehow makes them all the more delicious!

Instead of baking 12 separate buns, you can place the buns together before they bake, and then gently tear them apart. Eat warm, just as they are – or cold with a tiny smear of butter, freshly baked. Or, after a couple of days, they are wonderful split and toasted.

MAKES 12

500g/1 lb 2 oz/$4^{1}/_{3}$ cups unbleached strong white flour, sifted

1 teaspoon salt

40g/$1^{1}/_{2}$ oz/$^{1}/_{4}$ cup light muscovado sugar

$^{1}/_{2}$ teaspoon mixed spice

$^{1}/_{2}$ teaspoon ground cinnamon

55g/2 oz/$^{1}/_{2}$ stick unsalted butter, chilled, diced

100g/$3^{1}/_{2}$ oz/$^{2}/_{3}$ cup raisins and currants

25g/1 oz/2 tablespoons chopped mixed peel

7g/$^{1}/_{4}$ oz sachet of fast-action/easy-blend dried yeast

300ml/$^{1}/_{2}$ pint/$1^{1}/_{3}$ cups mixed milk and water, heated to tepid

FOR THE PASTRY AND GLAZE

70g/$2^{1}/_{2}$ oz/$^{2}/_{3}$ cup plain flour

40g/$1^{1}/_{2}$ oz/$^{1}/_{2}$ stick unsalted butter, chilled, diced

1 tablespoon golden syrup

1 Place the flour in a bowl, then stir in the salt, sugar and spices. Rub in the butter until it resembles breadcrumbs. Stir in the dried fruits and peel, then stir in the yeast. Slowly stir in the tepid liquid and bring the mixture together in your hands to form a ball. Turn out on to a floured surface and knead for 10 minutes.

2 Place in a lightly oiled bowl and cover with oiled clingfilm. Leave for about 2 hours (or $1^{1}/_{2}$ if your house is warmer than mine!) until well risen.

3 Lightly oil a baking sheet. Knock back the dough and divide into 12 pieces. Roll into balls and place on the prepared baking sheet. Put in a warm place for about 45 minutes or until well risen again. Meanwhile, preheat the oven to 220°C/425°F/Gas 7.

4 To make the pastry, place the flour in a bowl and rub in the butter. Slowly add enough cold water (1–$1^{1}/_{2}$ tablespoons) to combine to a stiff dough. Break into 24 pieces and roll out into long sausage shapes. Join two together to form 12 crosses. Place a cross over each risen bun, then bake for 18–20 minutes or until puffed up and golden brown.

5 While the buns are baking, gently melt the syrup in a microwave or a small pan over a low heat. Lift the buns on to a wire rack and brush the tops with the syrup. Leave to cool.

HALLOWE'EN BARM BRACK

One of the reasons I love barm brack is because it is so similar to Selkirk bannock, which I adore, though the latter is prepared first as a plain bread dough, then the add-ons – sultanas, peel and butter – are kneaded in after the initial rising. With this barm brack, everything is added at the beginning, so as you knead you have to keep poking the dried fruit back in, but that is all part of the fun!

Traditionally baked for Hallowe'en in a cast-iron pot (bastible) hung over an open fire, the name comes from the word 'barm' meaning the froth that collects on fermenting malt liquor, which was traditionally used before the introduction of baker's yeast. 'Brack' means 'speckled' – from the dried fruit and peel. According to Darina Allen's seminal book, *Irish Traditional Cooking*, at Hallowe'en small trinkets, such as coins, rings or thimbles, are wrapped in greaseproof paper and hidden in the loaf before baking, reminiscent of the coins similarly wrapped and put into Scots cloutie dumpling made for celebrations and birthdays.

Enjoy a slice of barm brack fresh or toasted with or without butter, but always with tea.

MAKES 1 LOAF

500g/1 lb 2 oz/4$\frac{1}{3}$ cups unbleached strong
white flour

1 teaspoon ground mixed spice

a tiny grating of nutmeg

7g/$\frac{1}{4}$ oz sachet of fast-action/easy-blend dried
yeast

1 teaspoon salt

50g/1$\frac{3}{4}$ oz/$\frac{1}{2}$ stick unsalted butter, diced

50g/1$\frac{3}{4}$ oz/$\frac{1}{4}$ cup golden caster sugar

150g/5$\frac{1}{2}$ oz/1 cup currants

50g/1$\frac{3}{4}$ oz/$\frac{1}{3}$ cup sultanas

50g/1$\frac{3}{4}$ oz/$\frac{1}{3}$ cup chopped mixed peel

300ml/$\frac{1}{2}$ pint/1$\frac{1}{3}$ cups tepid milk

1 tablespoon golden caster sugar, to glaze

1 Place the flour, spices, yeast and salt in a bowl, and rub in the butter. Stir in the sugar, dried fruits and peel, then pour in the milk. Once combined, turn out on to a floured surface and knead for 10 minutes until smooth. Place in a lightly oiled bowl, cover with oiled clingfilm and leave in a warm place for 2–3 hours until risen.

2 Lightly butter a deep, 20cm/8 in cake tin. Knock back the dough and shape into a round to fit the tin. Cover again and leave in a warm place for another hour or so until it has risen again. Meanwhile, preheat the oven to 220°C/425°F/Gas 7.

3 Bake for 15 minutes, then reduce the temperature to 200°C/400°F/Gas 6. Cook for a further 30–35 minutes. Loosely cover with foil during the last 15 minutes of cooking to prevent burning. The cake is cooked when it sounds hollow when tapped underneath.

4 To make the glaze, put 1 tablespoon water in a small pan and bring to the boil. Add the sugar and dissolve it over a low heat. Use this to brush over the top of the bread, then return it to the oven for 2 minutes. Remove from the tin to a wire rack to cool completely before slicing.

Useful contacts

ABERFELDY WATERMILL
For all grades of oatmeal.
Tel: +44 1887 820803

ALFORD OATMEAL
For all grades of oatmeal.
Tel: +44 1975 562209

ALAN SILVERWOOD LIMITED
Best brownie pan, heavy-duty girdles (griddles)
and lots more.
Tel: +44 121 454 3571

AU COMPTOIR DES CHEFS
Skinned raw pistachio nuts (i.e. shelled and
skinned – bright green) are not widely available
in the UK, but the Paris-based Au Comptoir des
Chefs (who also supply excellent chocolate)
do mail order.
Tel: +33 1 34 76 03 09
Or visit www.aucomptoirdeschefs.com

BILLINGTONS
The best selection of unrefined sugar.
Tel: +44 151 243 9056
Or visit www.billingtons.co.uk

CARRS FLOUR MILLS
Highly recommended flours for bread machines.
Tel: +44 1228 554600
Or visit www.carrs-flourmills.co.uk

CUCINADIRECT
Baking sheets/pans and fashionable tea
services.
Tel: 0870 420 4300
Or visit www.cucinadirect.com

DIVERTIMENTI
Baking equipment and stylish tableware.
33/34 Marylebone High Street,
London, W1U 4PT
Tel: +44 20 7935 0689
or
139/141 Fulham Road, London, SW3 6SD
Tel: +44 20 7581 8065
Or visit www.divertimenti.co.uk

DOVES FARM
Produces a wide range of organic flours suitable
for all baking.
Tel: +44 1488 684880
Or visit www.dovesfarm.co.uk

THE FLOUR BIN
Specialises in high-protein Canadian wheat
for breads.
Tel: +44 1246 860520
Or visit www.flourbin.com

GILLIES FINE FOODS
For superb jams all made from fruit grown in
the Scottish Highlands.
Tel: +44 1349 861100
Or visit www.gilliesfinefoods.co.uk

JANE ASHER CAKE AND SUGARCRAFT
Printed frosting sheets (for cake icing)
and sugarcraft items.
22/24 Cale Street, London, SW3 3QU
Tel: +44 20 7584 6177
Or visit www.jane-asher.co.uk

LAKELAND LIMITED
All the baking equipment you will ever need.
They also stock Silverwood's amazing brownie
pan with slide-out base.
Tel: +44 1539 488100
Or visit www.lakelandlimited.co.uk

SHIPTON MILL
For a wide range of stoneground flours.
Tel: +44 1666 505050
Or visit www.shipton-mill.com

Glossary of British/American baking terms

BRITISH	AMERICAN
Baking parchment	Parchment paper
Bicarbonate of soda	Baking soda
Black treacle	Molasses
Caster sugar	Superfine sugar
Clingfilm	Saran wrap
Coriander	Cilantro
Double cream	Heavy cream
Flat-leaf parsley	Italian parsley
Frying pan	Skillet
Granulated sugar	Table sugar
Greaseproof paper	Wax paper
Grill	Broil
Icing sugar	Confectioners' sugar
Plain flour	All-purpose flour
Polenta	Cornmeal
Self-raising flour	Self-rising flour
Single cream	Light cream
Skirt beef	Beef flank
Tin	Pan
Tin foil	Aluminum foil

Acknowledgements

Thanks to the following:
My parents, Anna and Bob Anderson; Barry and Jackie Barraclough; Maggie Beer; Joanna Blythman; Jimmy Burgess; Joan Bunting; Mary-An Charnley; Sally Clarke; Anna Del Conte; Mary Contini; Roz Denny; Linda Dick; Clarissa Dickson Wright; Anne Dow; Jill Dupleix; Lindsey Grieve; Jennifer and Elisabeth Hadden; Muriel Hadden and Bette Henderson; Scott and Sue Hadden; Christine Hall; Rhonda Hewitt; Heather Holden-Brown; Neil Honor; Margaret Horn; Fiona Hunter; Ingela Kassander; Stephan Kaptain; Hilary and John Lawrence; Mafe Marwick; Bill McLaren; John Mellis; Ritva Miettunen; Maureen Mills; Nick Nairn; Jill Norman; Bill Plews; Isabelle and Iain Plews; Chris Stevenson; Cornelius Van Hage; Colin Watson; Hilary Wheeler

Special thanks to Jo Roberts-Miller at Headline for her understanding and patience; Isobel Gillan for her innovative design; my agent Mary Pachnos; and to Maxine Clark for her brilliant food in the photos.

Thanks also to everyone at Billingtons, the unrefined sugar people (especially Ray, Joyce, Mark C., Mark B. and Emma) for all their support – and their fabulous sugars!

And finally, thanks to my dear family: Pat, Euan, Faith and Jessica – for eating yet more cake.

Index